DEFEATING
MAU MAU

L. S. B. Leakey

METHUEN & CO. LTD, LONDON
36 Essex Street, Strand, WC

Library of Congress Cataloging in Publication Data

Leakey, Louis Seymour Bazett, 1903-1972.
    Defeating Mau Mau.

    Reprint of the 1954 ed. published by Methuen,
London.
    1. Mau Mau. 2. Nationalism—Kenya.
I. Title.
DT433.575.L4   1977   967.6'203   74-15061
ISBN 0-404-12102-0

Reprinted from an original in the collections
of the Ohio State University Libraries

From the edition of 1954, London
First AMS edition published in 1977
Manufactured in the United States of America

AMS PRESS, INC.
NEW YORK, N.Y.

DEFEATING
MAU MAU

AMS PRESS
NEW YORK

PREFACE

Mau Mau is losing ground rapidly with the masses of the Kikuyu, but it would be foolish to attempt to predict when it will be completely defeated.

The means of defeating it are not only the use of arms manpower and physical warfare. Much more depends upon a full understanding of the reason why Mau Mau obtained such a hold on the people, how it was organised, and what must be done to alter the minds of the people who have been seduced by its false promises, and upon removing genuine grievances and causes of discontent.

Very serious consideration must also be given to the fact that Mau Mau became a religion and that other beliefs must now be made available to take the place of Mau Mau-ism, which is being abandoned by many who joined the movement.

While I am sure that the simple teachings of Christ can provide the answer for this, I am less sure that the Churches will be willing to free themselves from so much which is in their rules and which goes beyond fundamental Christianity. Some of these things have in the past been a stumbling block to many Africans who sincerely wished to follow Christ.

In this new book I have tried to provide material that will help to defeat Mau Mau, heal the mental wounds that have been inflicted upon all races in Kenya, and prevent similar outbreaks in the future.

While this book is complete in itself, a fuller picture can be obtained by also reading my earlier work *Mau Mau and the Kikuyu* in which I dealt with the background of Mau Mau.

L. S. B. L.

372 46

CONTENTS

I

THE PRESENT POSITION

When I wrote *Mau Mau and the Kikuyu* at the end of 1952, the State of Emergency in Kenya Colony had only recently been declared and the aim of that book was to give my readers an idea of the background against which the Mau Mau organisation and its deeds must be viewed, in order to be properly understood.

Now the fight against Mau Mau has been in progress for nearly two years and it is unfortunately true that very few people, outside Kenya, seem to realise what is really happening. Only major events, at relatively rare intervals, now figure in the world press, together with dissertations of varying length and widely different viewpoints, written by journalists and others, mostly after relatively brief visits to Kenya. Even the local newspapers report only a proportion of the daily incidents.

From time to time, in answer to questions in the House of Commons, a general statement of the position is made and some of the statistical facts about the number of killed, captured, imprisoned, and detained is given. These stark figures do go to show the terrible reality of the fight against Mau Mau, but even they are often misinterpreted by people outside Kenya, because of a lack of background against which they can be seen in their true perspective.

I hope therefore in the present book to try and give a fuller picture, not only of the position as it is today, but also of what has been happening in the past two years.

When the State of Emergency was declared on 20 October 1952, one of the first steps taken by Government was to arrest and put under detention almost 120 of the known leaders of the Mau Mau movement. These included Jomo

I

Kenyatta and a number of members of the Central Committee, as well as a large number of chairmen and vice-chairmen of district Committees both in the Kikuyu Native Land Units and in the up-country farming districts, and in the towns.

As we shall see when we discuss Mau Mau methods of organisation, this did not have quite the disrupting effect that was hoped for, because, under the system that was in force, each man had a deputy behind the scenes, and the moment the principals were arrested these deputies took on their duties (and, of course, appointed their own deputies, in case they in their turn should be arrested).

The Mau Mau organisation was, however, very far from ready for action in October 1952, and, at once, numbers of men who had been selected for 'active service' took themselves off to the forests on the slopes of Mount Kenya and the Aberdare Range, where intensive training was started, and hide-outs prepared.

Meanwhile Mau Mau's propaganda machine was put into full gear, young men were called upon to volunteer to join the fighting groups, while the intimidation gangs in the towns and also on the Native Land Units, started to attack loyalists much more openly than they had done before. The administration of the Mau Mau oath was speeded up and many new members recruited.

In the meantime the drive to obtain arms and ammunition supplies was also accelerated, since it was no longer necessary to be careful not to draw too much attention to activities in this direction.

Then came the start of the long-drawn-out trial of Jomo Kenyatta and five of those who were charged with him of being the principal organisers of Mau Mau—its management committee. The results of this trial have only just been finalised with the refusal of leave to appeal to the Privy Council in July 1954.

Of the five who were charged with Kenyatta, one—the

Luo member—was acquitted on appeal to the Supreme Court of Kenya (although he had been sentenced by the magistrate with the others in the lower court). The others, with Jomo Kenyatta, are now serving their sentence of seven years' hard labour.

The trial was a memorable one in many ways. The defence was in the hands of Mr. Pritt, Q.C., with other learned counsel to help him, and the prosecution in the able hands of Mr. A. Somerhaugh assisted by Mr. John Webber. The fearless way in which the many Kikuyu witnesses for the Crown gave their evidence, created a very strong impression upon all those who attended the sessions.

The trial dragged on several weary months and many persons were called as defence witnesses, who were already detained for their part in the movement. At one stage proceedings were adjourned while leading Counsel was called upon to answer a charge of contempt of court—on which he was acquitted.

As time went on and as the Mau Mau followers who had retired to the forest for training began to be ready for action, the second phase started, with many well-planned raids by the gangsters on farms, police posts, and upon loyalist Kikuyu villages.

Government realised that it had very inadequate forces to deal with the situation and further troops from England were sent to supplement those who had arrived at the time the State of Emergency was declared.

A number of brutal attacks were made upon European families, and women and children and elderly people were among those killed, but the total number of incidents involving Europeans was very small, for the directions of the Mau Mau leaders was to concentrate attacks upon loyalist members of the tribe, in order to intimidate them (and any others who thought of helping the Government) into at least a state of passivity. In this

3

they had not, however, succeeded as much as they had hoped.

When Government decided that a large number of Kikuyu employed in the European farming areas must be moved away, and sent back to the Native Land Unit, for security reasons, thousands of others decided to go without waiting for orders to do so.

This voluntary move was accelerated by the fact that Government decided to introduce a new system of identity cards for all Kikuyu outside the Native Land Unit, cards which had to carry a photograph of the owner. This measure was very strongly opposed by Mau Mau leaders—who realised the disadvantage to their followers of easy and quick identification—and in obedience to orders from Mau Mau H.Q. very many, at first, refused to be photographed, preferring to be jailed for defiance of a lawful order.

When Mau Mau leaders realised that nothing could prevent the order from being enforced, they quickly organised a system for issuing forged identity cards; this counter measure was so successfully carried out that, recently, Government has been forced to introduce a new (and more forgery-proof) passport book system.

This book is not intended to provide a detailed history of events in the fight against Mau Mau, the time will come later for that to be compiled. The object rather is to show how Mau Mau organised itself, how it persuaded the masses to join in with it, and what were its aims.

I have recently had the privilege of long conversations with very many leaders of Kikuyu opinion, most of whom were old friends of mine (but a few of whom I was meeting for the first time), while they were in Nairobi to draft and broadcast an appeal to the tribe. All of them confirmed the view that I have held for several months, that *because* the masses are now swinging away from Mau Mau, we must expect, during the next few months, and certainly before

4

what I am writing here is actually published, a considerable increase in deeds of violence. As the masses more and more refuse to give either active or passive help to the gangsters, so will the latter, in proportion, become more desperate and try hard, by new acts of intimidation and violence, to turn the tide back in their favour.

Since, in this opening chapter, I want to give my readers a better idea of the position as it is today, I propose to start with a series of quotations from recent issues of the leading local newspaper, *The East African Standard*. I have purposely not been selective in this, I have simply taken the issues of the paper for a random period of six days from Friday, 29 January to Thursday, 4 February. When reading these extracts it must be remembered that this was not an unusual week, in any way, in the fight against Mau Mau. This sort of thing has been going on each and every day—often with much blacker weeks than this—for the past twenty months.

From the issue of Friday, 29 January 1954:

'A Home Guard patrol, led by a District Officer, Mr. Harry Hinde, and an Agricultural Officer, Mr. Victor Burke, discovered a mobile Mau Mau gun factory in the Meru forest near Kibiricho, G.H.Q. East Africa reported yesterday.

'The Home Guard, from the Muriga location of Meru, found twelve terrorists working on guns. Two Mau Mau sentries fired at the patrol which included five agricultural inspectors and tribal police. In returning the fire Chief Heman wounded one of the sentries. The gangsters fled. In their hide-out were thirteen partly-made guns, binoculars, springs, nuts and bolts, tools, ammunition, Mau Mau documents and clothing.'

'Mortar bombs and some home-made guns and shotgun cartridges were recovered from terrorists in the Eastern Aberdares.'

5

'A gang of six, armed with four home-made guns, raided a *duka* five miles east of Kiambu. The owner and his wife and two Kikuyu Guard were abducted and £40 stolen. All, except one of the Kikuyu Guard, escaped. He was found murdered a few miles away.'

'A Kikuyu Guard patrol attacked a gang of sixteen in the South Nyeri Reserve and inflicted casualties. Four prisoners and a home-made rifle and ammunition were captured.'

'A patrol of the 7th K.A.R. were ambushed about twelve miles east of Nyeri by a gang armed with an automatic and other fire-arms. The terrorists fled when the patrol fired back.'

'A European reported that his car was fired at on the Kijabe road but no damage was done. An Asian was wounded when a vehicle was ambushed near Embu by a gang of four. One terrorist was killed. The other three escaped.'

'A Police patrol in the residential area of the Bernhard Estate, off Sclaters Road, Nairobi, opened fire on two Africans who refused to halt when challenged on Wednesday night. One of the men was wounded and both were arrested.'

PISTOLS STOLEN FROM CARS: OWNERS FINED

'Miss Barbara Allen, aged 21, was fined 400/- in Nairobi District Commissioner's Court for failing to keep her pistol in safe custody. She left the pistol in a box on the back seat of her car in Nairobi, it was stated. She locked the doors, but one of the windows was slightly open and, although she was away from the car for less than five minutes, the window was forced and the gun was stolen.'

'Following the theft of a pistol and sixteen rounds of ammunition from an unlocked car parked outside

6

the New Stanley Hotel, a European woman, Miss B. Joffe of Nanyuki, was fined 400/- by a Nairobi magistrate.'

From the issue of 30 January 1954:

'A member of the Medical Department, Kisumu, R. B. Highton, was fined 500/- by the Resident Magistrate, Mr. I. Rosen, for failing to keep ammunition in safe custody. It was stated that Highton left twenty-five rounds of ammunition in a briefcase, which disappeared from his car when he left it for five minutes.'

'A Luo, Gilbert Adada s/o Nyambok from Asembo, charged before the Kisumu Resident Magistrate with being a member of the Mau Mau at first denied the charge. Later he changed his plea, and said "I will tell the truth—I am a member of the Mau Mau". He was sentenced to twelve months' hard labour.'

'Special Branch officers operating in bush country south of Nairobi have recovered two home-made .303 rifles and an assortment of ammunition. The finds are being followed up.'

'Another Mau Mau arms factory has been found—this time a few miles east of Thika, G.H.Q. East Africa reported yesterday.

'There were sixteen partly-made guns in the factory which a patrol of the 156 H.A.A. Battery discovered. Four terrorists were captured and other casualties were inflicted.'

'When Chief Ndungu's *boma* was attacked by a gang between 15 and 20 strong, a Kikuyu Guard was wounded and eight huts were burned down.'

'A police patrol contacted a gang of forty at Bush Sawmill on the North Kinangop and recovered a quantity of clothing and food.'

'Five of a gang of twenty-five were killed by a police patrol from Sekutiak in the Masai Reserve. A .303 rifle was also captured.'

'Some terrorists were wounded when a patrol attacke 1 a large gang in the Gatundu Location. The gang : hide-out was also found and a prisoner was taken. A home-made rifle and a large quantity of food and clothing were captured.'

'One home-made rifle and some ammunition were recovered by a patrol of the 7th K.A.R. which contacted a gang in the Magutu Location. One terrorist was wounded and another captured, but he later escaped. Several other casualties were inflicted.'

'In the Resident Magistrate's Court, Nakuru, J. G. Joubert was fined 1,000/- for having left ten rounds of .303 ammunition in an unlocked car. The car was left on a farm in the Solai area.'

From the issue of 1 February 1954:

'Special Branch officers recovered 215 rounds of ammunition when they raided an empty Mau Mau hide-out in the Muthaiga area.'

'A gang of about ten terrorists armed with two rifles and two pistols was sighted about ten miles north-west of Thika but they fled into thick bush when security forces tried to attack them, G.H.Q. East Africa reported yesterday.'

'Two home-made guns and the parts of several others were captured by a patrol of the 6th K.A.R. in the forest about fifteen miles north-east of Kijabe.'

'Two Kikuyu were found strangled in the Chui Estate in the Thika area. An automatic pistol was found in the labour lines of the Twiga Estate, also in the Thika district.'

'Kimani s/o Mwaniki, a terrorist wanted for the murder of an Embu Guard and two young children, was one of the two gangsters killed when patrols of the Embu Guard, K.P.R. and the K.A.R. contacted a small gang about two miles east of Embu in the Gaturi location. One terrorist was captured and a woman with the gang brought in for interrogation.'

'The Mguthige Guard post in the Meru area was attacked but although the post was partially burned down the defenders suffered no casualties.'

'A home-made rifle and fourteen rounds of ammunition were recovered from some terrorists in a large operation by Police, Kikuyu Guard and members of the 23rd K.A.R. in the Kirimukuyu location of South Nyeri. In the same location a police patrol wounded four members of a gang and captured eleven rounds of ammunition.

'Two suspected oath administrators were detained in the Molo district.'

From the issue of 2 February 1954:
'The maximum sentence, a fine of £100 with the alternative of three months' simple imprisonment, was imposed by Mr. E. D. Emley, First-Class Nairobi Magistrate, yesterday on a 23-year-old European, L. Powell of Nairobi, for an arms offence.
'Powell pleaded guilty to failing to take reasonable precautions to ensure that a firearm and ammunition were not stolen or made available to any person not lawfully entitled to possess them.

'It was stated that Powell on January 29th had a .25 automatic pistol and five rounds of ammunition loose in his coat pocket.

'Later he placed the coat with the weapon and ammunition on the seat of his car which he locked and then left. The fire-arm and ammunition were stolen.'

'An unsuccessful attempt to rob the Khalsa School, Racecourse Road, Nairobi, of £900 was made by an armed gang of four Africans yesterday.

'The gang walked into the school at about 10.45 a.m. and went into the principal's office where the secretary was counting the month's wages. The secretary screamed for help and two shots were fired at her but both missed.

'When the principal ran to his secretary's aid the gang rushed out. Two men were later detained.'

'A Kikuyu was found shot in the back near the Goan Institute in Juja Road, Eastleigh yesterday. He was not wounded seriously.'

'A Seychellois was robbed of a gun in Eastleigh yesterday and a rifle was stolen from a car on a farm near Thika.'

From the issue of 3 February 1954:

'At the end of a two-day hearing, the three African assessors at the trial of Waruhui s/o Itote, alias "General China" expressed the opinion that he was guilty of consorting with persons carrying fire-arms. Two of the assessors found him guilty of being in possession of two rounds of ammunition without lawful authority or excuse.

'Shown a letter dated December 28th last and addressed to another African, accused agreed that it bore his signal and stamp "General China, H.Q. Mount Kenya". The letter contained the sentence "I inform you to send charcoals and other things".

'Mr. Somerhaugh: "Is charcoals the Mau Mau trade name for ammunition?" "Yes."'

'Ten Kikuyu, two of whom are alleged to have administered the Mau Mau oath, were arrested at Mariashoni, near Molo, by police of the Molo Special Branch. Another four of the group are alleged to have taken the oath. It is considered probable by the police that a hard-core gang is lurking in the vicinity.'

'A police report from Thomson's Falls says that the search continues in the Rumuruti swamp, because it is believed that more terrorists were killed in the recent engagement in the area than had at first been realised.'

'On Muller's farm a police ambush contacted a gang of four, two of whom were armed with rifles. They wounded one member of the gang. Another gang stole cattle from a North Kinangop farm and attacked a nearby camp. Security forces returned fire and dispersed the attackers.'

'A sweep in the Kilimani area of Nairobi by units of the 6th K.A.R. rounded up 700 Africans. Seventy-five were detained for further questioning.'

'A Meru tribesman, M'Amwamba s/o M'Mwitari, has been sentenced to death on a charge of murder at the Supreme Court Emergency Assizes at Meru. 'He was a member of a gang which killed a Meru teacher and seriously injured his wife on the day after their wedding.'

From the issue of 4 February 1954:

'Eight Kikuyu and two Embu tribesmen were hanged at Nairobi Prison yesterday. Six had been sentenced in connection with the illegal possession of fire-arms and the others for murder.'

'Two police askaris were wounded—one of them fatally—when a well-armed terrorist gang was attacked near Rumuruti by police and troops with armoured cars. Two terrorists were taken, but one later escaped. A Verey-light pistol, ammunition and two home-made guns were captured. The gang was armed with a Sten-gun and at least one service rifle.'

'In the South Nyeri Reserve two African women were shot by terrorists and two others abducted.'

'Four men were abducted by a gang which attacked Kiruga. Blankets and clothing were stolen.'

'Women were among a large gang which destroyed some loyalist huts in Location 4 of Fort Hall.'

'Four home-made rifles, tools and spare parts were captured by a police patrol from a gang about ten miles south-east of Thika.'

'All the 2,300 men and women in the all-Kikuyu Bihati Location were rounded up when police and military screened the location on Tuesday.'

'An African woman stopped a passing "999" car in Victoria Street, Nairobi, and said she had seen a man carrying a pistol. She toured the area in the patrol car and spotted the man but he was not carrying the gun when the police stopped him. He was however detained for screening.'

'An African Mbarire, alias "Major Blue", has been sentenced to death at Nyeri Emergency Assize Court for possessing a home-made gun and fourteen rounds of ammunition. He was arrested in Mugutu Location on December 20th.'

'A Sten-gun with two loaded magazines and £1,000 in cash were stolen when a Forest Department Land Rover, in which two Europeans and three Africans were travelling, was ambushed in the Mount Kenya Forest Reserve on Tuesday afternoon. The vehicle was brought to a halt about two miles south-west of Ndathi by shots. One shattered the windscreen. There were no casualties.'

'An armed gang of about twenty Africans drove in two lorries to the Verjee Petrol Station, in Buckley Road, on the edge of the Nairobi Industrial Area early yesterday, broke open the stores and stole several hundred pounds worth of goods.'

'Two pistols were recovered by police yesterday—one at Thika, where a Kikuyu with it in his possession was arrested, and the other at Kiambu.'

'Three Africans were arrested yesterday within three minutes of allegedly robbing with violence an Asian, Mrs. Jella Gulam, at her home in Third Avenue, Parklands.'

In spite of the appalling state of affairs revealed by this summary of the reports for only six days, it would be wrong if the impression were given that Mau Mau is as strong now as it has been at various times in the past. Nearly every one who is in close contact with what is happening is agreed that, *so far as the masses are concerned*, there is a very noticeable swing away from Mau Mau and in favour of the forces of law and order. Information on gang movements and other activities is being brought in more than ever before, and reports from accurate sources show that there is an increasing rift between rival leaders, both in the gangs and in the general organisation.

This of course in turn means that as the real hard-core become more desperate—for funds, for food supplies, and for manpower—so will they indulge in greater deeds of violence in desperation, in the hope of turning the tide of Kikuyu opinion back in their favour.

In the meantime the real out and out Mau Mau leaders are also doing more and more to try and win over other tribes in Kenya to their cause. There is evidence that they have succeeded with many individuals in other tribes and in certain 'black spots' in other tribal areas, their influence seems to be affecting the people more deeply and there are signs of a real organisation developing—the counterpart of Mau Mau. But if the present trend away from sympathy with Mau Mau continues, among the Kikuyu, then these attempts to influence other tribes will also lose their efficacy.

There is, however, a very real new danger present today. If Mau Mau, by means of some major success against the Security Forces, managed to win back their wavering prestige, then serious acts of violence might break out in other tribal areas where they have been desperately trying to instil their poison.

Then too, over the closing months of 1953 Mau Mau succeeded in winning over thousands of Kikuyu in neighbouring territories like Tanganyika, where the Government has had to take drastic steps to nip the movement in the bud. The potential danger from this spread of Mau Mau outside Kenya is very great and should not be underestimated, for it would be relatively easy—by giving a false picture of what Mau Mau is—to win over the sympathy of tribes in other territories who really have no possible interest in what Mau Mau does or does not do.

During January and February of 1954 certain events of considerable significance have taken place in connection with the fight against Mau Mau, events which I think clearly show the trend of events and which augur well for the future.

In January a group of twenty-three Kikuyu leaders met together in Nairobi for joint discussions on how to bring the Mau Mau terror to an end, and how to accelerate the swing away from the terrorists which they all agreed had started. This group included Government Chiefs who have been in the forefront of the physical fight against the gangsters, two Kikuyu members of Legislative Council, five African Ministers of Religion (who have played a great part in leading the Christians in their resistance to the wickedness of Mau Mau), and a number of Kikuyu political leaders of moderate and progressive views.

The men came not only from all three districts of Kikuyu country—Kiambu, Fort Hall and Nyeri—but also from Embu and from Nairobi and from places in the White Highlands where Kikuyu have for years resided as labour. It was, I believe, the first time, at any rate for very many years, that the leaders in such a wide field of thought and activity had met for full and frank discussion. In the past there had been a growing tendency for Church leaders to

14

meet alone and for political leaders to be rather frowned
upon by Government Chiefs and their views not welcomed.
But now, drawn together by a common desire to see their
people and their land freed from the terrible consequences
of Mau Mau, they met.

The principal reason for their meeting was to prepare
an agreed statement calling on all Kikuyu to have nothing
more to do with Mau Mau. The appeal which they drew
up in Kikuyu has been translated and is as follows:

'We who are speaking to you today are, all of us,
well-known as leaders of the African people here in
Kenya.

'Some of us are members of Legislative Council,
others are Chiefs, others again are Church leaders, and
others are leaders of organisations which aim to put
forward the views of the people of our country, and we
have come together from the whole country from Ngong
to Meru.

'Now we all wish to speak to you with one voice
and in complete unanimity, because of the very evil
things which are ruining our country. It is because we
have seen for ourselves the wickedness that is being
perpetrated by the leaders of Mau Mau and by those
who follow them, that we wish first to remind you of
some of these evils which have brought nothing but
distress in their train, in order that each one of you
yourselves may think seriously about these things and
abandon them for good.

'First of all we would remind you that the things which
are being done by Mau Mau at this time have caused
hatred between Kikuyu and Kikuyu, between many
Kikuyu and Government and between the Kikuyu and
the other inhabitants of Kenya.

'As you yourselves well know, this evil organisation
which is called Mau Mau had administered oaths unto
the people, oaths which are completely at variance with
Kikuyu custom. Some have taken these oaths voluntarily,
others have been forced into taking them or have taken

15

them because they have been persuaded to do so under the enticement of false promises.

'And because of these oaths, which are evil, those who have taken them voluntarily have committed crimes such as have never been seen before as you yourselves well know: wanton murder, robbery, massacre, slashing stock, destroying crops, and burning people in their houses. Furthermore, you are aware of the way in which these evil people mutilate people and have been drinking the blood and eating the meat of those whom they have slaughtered.

'Moreover, very many people who have taken this Mau Mau oath, even though they did so involuntarily, have also done evil deeds as a result of fear, and have been unwilling to reveal the secrets of those who have administered the oath unto them by force, or to reveal their secret deeds. But we say you have no need either to fear or to believe in these oaths for they cannot bring harm to anybody since they have not been administered in accordance with the lawful customs of the people. The lawful oaths of the Kikuyu are administered by the elders in broad daylight; they are not administered to women and children and, moreover, nobody may take a lawful oath until he has first informed his family of his wish to do so and has received their consent.

'Further, we say the leaders of Mau Mau and those who have followed them have introduced a new doctrine of their own which attacks the true religion of Christianity. They have introduced, in fact, a doctrine which is of utter wickedness but which they deceive you by calling a religion.

'You know well that Mau Mau and its followers have burnt down very many schools; have killed or mutilated many teachers and also school children, and have, further, put a ban on children attending schools. There is no race that can make proper progress without education.

'Then again, the leaders of Mau Mau and those who follow them have closed the doors on the gaining of wealth by the Kikuyu people—their trade, their looking after cattle and their agriculture—until now the whole country is full of poverty and many children have practically nothing to eat or clothes in which to dress themselves. It has even come to pass that when a woman sells a little maize or some other produce for a few cents she has to donate what she gets to collectors and her money does not benefit the children, yet no one knows what happens to the money that is so contributed.

'Furthermore, because of the evil deeds of violence that have been done by Mau Mau very many people have been killed, very many more have been imprisoned, very many have been moved from their rightful homes and have had to abandon all they possessed. What is the profit of all this? It is nothing but pure terror that has been brought upon you by Mau Mau. They have taken away, but they have given back nothing.

'Furthermore, because of the wicked deeds of the Mau Mau leaders and their followers, those who wish to speak on behalf of their country truthfully are not listened to any more and they have been robbed of any chance of doing anything to help you.

'Moreover, at this time and because of this evil, very many people have left their legitimate work which brought them profit and have gone to dwell in the forests like wild beasts. They state that they are seeking self-government for the Kikuyu when, in fact, all they are doing is to destroy the Kikuyu people.

'What profit would there possibly be in being ruled by people who perform such wicked deeds and yet there are still some of you who are actively helping the forest gangs; what possible good do they ever do for you?

'We say unto you unitedly and with utter conviction that as we see it self-government could never be achieved by such methods as those of massacre and murder; nay, the time for self-government is simply being put further and further back; self-government will only come by complete agreement between all the people of Kenya of all races unitedly.

'And now, because of these evil deeds that we have listed for you our country has reached a very sorry state and is retrogressing instead of making progress, and the case of the Kikuyu people has lost all honour. We therefore are going to tell you more of the things which you all can do in order that peace may be restored.

'Firstly, we speak unto you who have gone into the bush and the forests. You should, here and now, come out and surrender to Government before you are utterly destroyed, for assuredly if you do not surrender you will, without doubt, be killed.

'Secondly, we say unto those of you who dwell amongst us but help those pirates by giving them food, by giving them shelter, by giving them money and by helping them in other ways, we say unto you—cease to give them any help; cease immediately in order that peace and good works may return to us.

'Thirdly, we say unto you who sit on the fence and who are neither on our side of it or the other and do not know where you are—come over immediately on the side of those who want peace, help Government and cease to be deceived by Mau Mau.

'Fourthly, we say unto you who have fought and are fighting still for the truth, that your name is held in high regard by Government as well as by the women and children whom you are helping to protect, and we say unto you—do not grow tired in the fight; stand firmly that together we may bring this present strife to an end.

'Fifthly, we say to every one of you, great and small— do everything in your power to help to bring back peace quickly by giving information against those who do these evil deeds:
- (a) by giving information against the gangsters and wherever you see them;
- (b) by going and reporting whenever you hear that oath ceremonies are going to take place, and revealing where they will be;
- (c) by going and reporting whenever you know they have been or are stealing crops or raiding stock;
- (d) by revealing the places where they hide their weapons, and where they hide themselves; and

(*e*) by refusing utterly to comply when they demand
    funds or food or any other assistance from you.

'Because of your wickedness and your many sins
Government has rightly declared that those who are the
real leaders of Mau Mau will never be allowed to return
to Kikuyu country again.

'Finally, we say unto all of you wherever you may be
as you listen to us, great and small, men, women and
children—the time has come when you must have
nothing more to do with this Mau Mau gangsterism;
we call upon you to come, one and all, on the side of those
who want peace in order that our Government may
again start upon the path of progress, for assuredly
it has been put backwards very seriously.

'Let us all, therefore, unite with Government and with
all those who want peace that this country of Kenya
may once more become a land of peace and of wealth
and of progress.'

This meeting had far wider and greater significance
than the mere issue of a united call to abandon Mau Mau.
Out of this joint discussion, which lasted more than twenty-
four hours, there appeared a remarkable unanimity of view
on all sorts of other matters affecting their people, and before
the delegates went back to their respective homes they
had an interview with the Member for Native Affairs and
submitted a large number of very reasonable requests to
him, for the consideration of Government.

Not the least significant fact was that they decided that
in future such meetings of leaders, *drawn from all walks of life*
and from the whole Kikuyu area, should be held at relatively
frequent intervals, because they all felt that it had
been of the greatest benefit to meet in the way they had
done.

There was another very interesting event which arose as
a direct consequence of the meeting of Kikuyu leaders.
After the conference they unanimously asked the Governor
to arrange for an informal conference between leaders of

the African, European, and the Asian communities to discuss what further steps could be taken by all to combat Mau Mau and to restore peace.

This meeting took place on 15 February, and was probably the first time that political leaders of all the main races in Kenya had ever met together in this way, or to such good purpose.

If this precedent is followed up, the auguries for the future will be much improved.

II

MAU MAU AIMS

There has never, so far as I know, been any clearly enunciated statement of the aims of the Mau Mau organisation. Indeed, the leaders have, to a considerable extent, when making speeches, modified their words to suit the particular audience they were addressing. Thus, when speaking to an audience that included many Christians, the aim of abolishing Christianity was not mentioned, while stress was laid on the aim of 'getting back the stolen lands', without too much emphasis on how this was to be achieved by murder and violence, which would be abhorrent to their listeners.

Broadly speaking, however, it is possible to get a very good overall picture of Mau Mau aims by studying their published propaganda, both in the form of the 'hymn books', which we shall consider in some detail, in the published speeches of leaders and in 'Letters to the Editor' published in the vernacular press, before the Emergency was declared.

The aims can be briefly summarised under the following seven headings:

1. Recover the land stolen from us by the white man.
2. Obtain self-government.
3. Destroy Christianity.
4. Restore ancient customs whenever possible.
5. Drive out, or subjugate, all foreigners.
6. Abolish soil conservation.
7. Increase secular education.

It will be valuable, I think, to consider each of these headings separately in order to see why it was an aim of the movement.

21

1. *Recover the land stolen by the white man*

For the Kikuyu the land is indubitably the most sacred thing. To him it is at once 'his mother and father', his most sacred possession and the foundation stone of all prosperity. It is, as I made clear in my earlier book on the Mau Mau, a matter of history that, owing to the combination of a set of unusual circumstances, the Kikuyu did lose a certain amount of their tribal land, by alienation to Europeans, in the early years of the century.

I have tried to make it clear that what was done was done in good faith, but with much misunderstanding on *both sides*, and also that, in any event, the amount of Kikuyu land that was so alienated was infinitesimal, compared with what remained in their possession.

An opportunity to make amends for the genuine wrong that was done to a section of the Kikuyu in respect of their land, was provided when the Morris Carter Land Commission was appointed. Had the leaders of Kikuyu thought put their claims before that Commission in an honest and reasonable manner, I have no doubt at all that the Commission would have recommended adequate compensation.

As it was, however, the leaders of the Kikuyu Central Association, who were then the most active Kikuyu political party, did not do this. Instead, they encouraged those members of their tribe who had genuinely lost land to the white man, to put in such preposterous claims—so exceeding the true facts—that it was inevitable that a clear-headed, judicial-minded body would reject the claims as too fantastic to be treated seriously. The issue was, in fact, so confused by the untrue evidence that was put forward that, in the end, the extent of the claims which the Commission finally accepted as genuine, fell far short—both in my opinion and in that of many others who knew the position—of reality.

Although this is all, now, past history, it must not be

forgotten that it left the Kikuyu masses in a state of grave discontent.

The leaders of the Kikuyu Central Association were not slow to make capital out of what happened and to turn it to their own ends. Mau Mau, as the successor of the Kenya Central Association when that body was declared unlawful—continued the same policy under almost identical leadership.

But the just and genuine land grievances of the Kikuyu were quite insufficient to stir up the degree of anger against the white man that Mau Mau wished to engender. It, therefore, became necessary to falsify history for the benefit of the growing generations and to tell the youth of the tribe that other land—which had never been in Kikuyu possession and which was now in European ownership—was also land that had once been Kikuyu property and had been 'stolen' from them.

We know, only too well, from the evidence of Nazi Germany how a lie, repeated often enough, finally becomes accepted as the truth. This is what indeed happened and by 1950 there were thousands of the younger generation of Kikuyu who had come to believe—absolutely—that the greater part of the 'White Highlands', the land in occupation by Europeans in Kenya, had formerly been Kikuyu land.

Having once succeeded in fostering this wholly false belief, the enormity of the crime of the white man in robbing the Kikuyu of all the best land, which was alleged to have been formerly theirs, became a rankling sore. By making 'the recovery of the land stolen by the European' its first and major aim, the Mau Mau movement thus had sure and certain means of winning a vast amount of support for what appeared to be a 'just and righteous cause'.

But there was another reason why the recovery of the land was one of the major aims enunciated by Mau Mau.

23

The political leaders of the movement were well aware that they could not hope to proceed with their plans without ample funds. They also knew that the one thing for which the Kikuyu will always gladly part with their money, is on a land issue. Again and again, in the days before 1939, whenever the Kikuyu Central Association leaders had announced that they were 'preparing a petition about the land that had been taken by the Europeans' and that 'funds were urgently needed in connection with the expenses of the petition', money had poured in to their offices. This financial help had come not only from those who had genuinely lost some land, but from hundreds of Kikuyu sympathisers, living in parts of Kikuyu country which had never been touched by alienation.

As the Mau Mau movement progressed and as more and more funds were needed, the use of 'land', as a major touchstone for money raising, was carried one step farther. Thousands of Kikuyu parted with money they could ill afford, when they were told that, if they did so, their names would be added to the lists of those who would share in the dividing up of the White Highlands after the Europeans had left, but that, if they did not contribute, then they would not be entitled to any share.

2. *Obtain self-government*

Whereas the recovery of the stolen lands was the primary plank in the Mau Mau platform—one stemming from a genuine internal grievance, magnified deliberately to suit political ends—the aim of achieving self-government which recurs again and again—*ad nauseum*—in all Mau Mau propaganda, was one of very different origin.

The achievement of self-government was never an active aim of the old Kikuyu Central Association, it was something which had not really ever been considered as being within the realms of possibility, in the earlier days. But the

Kikuyu have, for years, paid a great deal of attention to world news and they awakened, during the war years and in the years that followed, to the world-wide movements of peoples towards self-government. India and Pakistan 'obtained self-government' and 'threw off the English yoke'. The Gold Coast obtained self-government, so did Burma. Abyssinia had been helped by the British Empire (and by many East African natives, including Kikuyu, who served in the campaign) to return to self-government and throw off the Italian yoke. Self-government was in the air and was a much-talked-of subject among all that section of the Kikuyu that was literate enough to read the English, Swahili, or vernacular press.

In particular, the Kikuyu heard much from the Indians in Kenya of the blessings that had come to India and Pakistan through becoming independent. It was, therefore, almost inevitable that 'self-government' should be made a plank in the Mau Mau platform: one that was certain to attract a certain type of semi-educated, discontented Kikuyu to the cause. Moreover, 'self-government' was clearly understood to be something that could not be achieved without sacrifice and often bloodshed. So much was evident from world news. If, therefore, the idea of 'achieving self-government' could be successfully 'sold' to the Kikuyu masses as a Mau Mau aim, an inevitable corollary in the minds of the people would be that that goal could certainly only be achieved at the expense of death and bloodshed and violence. Thus the ground was skilfully prepared, in the minds of at least a part of the Kikuyu people, for a campaign of violence and actual fighting.

3. *Destroy Christianity*

At the time (in 1929 and onwards) when the Christian Missions were making a strong stand against the custom known as 'female circumcision' and were requiring their adherents to renounce it, the Kikuyu Central Association was one of the organisations that was most bitterly opposed to the Mission policy. The immediate outcome of the controversy, however, was not any direct attack upon Christianity but only upon the form of Christianity that was taught by the Missions. In consequence we saw the setting up of two major Independent Christian Church movements. The African Orthodox Church of Kenya and the Kikuyu Independent Pentecostal Church. Both of these movements started out with the idea of retaining the Christian religion, but in a form which the founders held to be more directly in accordance with the teaching of the Bible than the Mission rules and regulations that were part of the Christian teaching of the Missionaries.

An attack on the Christian faith was not ever contemplated at that time, although there was a great deal of verbal attack on the Christian foreign missions. Gradually, however, the subversive politicians came to realise that Christianity, in any form, was a barrier to the fulfilment of their aims and objects. Those who believed in Christianity —even if it was not the Mission form of that religion—still objected to violence, to lying and to other things which the politicians wished to foster. In consequence, efforts were made to transform some of the Independent Churches into places of instruction in a new religion which had nothing to do with the teachings of Christ—the Mau Mau religion. The denunciation of Christianity in any form was accelerated.

When a new Christian revival movement, known variously as 'Dini ya Ruanda' and 'Ahonoku', came into being, the threat to the actions of Mau Mau was much increased, because those who became members of the revival group were infinitely more outspoken in their attack upon the methods of the subversive politicians than any nominal or half-hearted Mission adherents. In consequence, it became customary to include a clause in the Mau Mau oath, directed, in so many words, against Christianity and in particular against membership of the 'Revival movement'.

From then on, it became increasingly common for Mau Mau propaganda to be openly 'anti-Christian'. This meant, of course, that it was no longer possible to do anything to win over the Christians by kind words and verbal inducements. The method of violence and threatened violence was therefore instituted instead.

It is probable that the inclusion of anti-Christian propaganda in the Mau Mau aims did more to crystallise opposition to the movement than anything else. Until this was done, there were a good many Christians who were so influenced by the propaganda about land and self-government that they were prepared to support Mau Mau and keep one eye shut to some of the things that were being done in its name. Once, however, 'destroy Christianity' became one of the watchwords of Mau Mau, and once (as a corollary) the turning of Mau Mau into a religion with its own heretical creed was openly known, the opinion of thousands of Christians 'hardened. They renounced all support of the movement and began to fight against it and oppose it openly.

4. *Restore ancient customs*

The use of this theme in propaganda has never been whole-hearted, and it is doubtful if any Mau Mau leader has ever dared to suggest a complete reversion to ancient customs. But as a rallying call it was useful, especially when accent was placed upon such things as 'polygamy', upon initiation ceremonies, and upon sacrifices to the ancestral spirits.

The more ardent Mau Mau leaders also tried to include under this heading the prohibition of smoking cigarettes, of drinking English brewed beer, and the wearing of hats, but they soon found that this side of the suggested return

27

to ancient customs had much less appeal, although the prohibition of English beer was maintained.

Although it was unpopular, when a ban was placed by Mau Mau on the wearing of hats and upon smoking cigarettes, thousands obeyed. In fact, the ban was not only observed by those who belonged to the movement but by very many Kikuyu loyalists as well. In the latter case, they did so in order not to draw too much attention to themselves as opponents of the movement.

The time came in fact, when, in places like Nairobi, it was not safe for any Kikuyu to wear a hat or smoke in public, no matter how much he hated Mau Mau, as to do so was to invite dire punishment and even death.

Although the slogan 'Return to Ancient Customs' was a useful one, in certain ways it has never been really pressed home. Indeed, in respect of all Mau Mau oath ceremonies, the tendency has been to do things which are in direct contradiction to established Kikuyu law and custom. It has, therefore, been possible to use this contradiction between the professed Mau Mau aim of restoring ancient customs and the wholly contradictory Mau Mau actions as a useful counter-propaganda weapon.

5. *Drive out all foreigners*

This aim, which appears again and again in Mau Mau propaganda, was always accompanied by statements pointing out the contrast between the wealth and life of comfort of the Europeans and the poverty and discomfort of the Africans. As a policy it was closely linked with the first aim of 'Recovery of Land', for, obviously, if the European farmers remained, they would not voluntarily give up the land they occupied and let it pass into Kikuyu hands, particularly when most of it was land that never had been Kikuyu country.

The benefits which the Europeans had brought to the

country in the form of education, technical knowledge, and medical aid, were all well known and well appreciated, so that in making the eviction of all Europeans one of the aims of the movement, the leaders again and again found themselves faced with serious difficulties in debate. These they overcame by saying that another of their aims was greatly increased education for all Kikuyu, which would enable the Kikuyu to fulfil all the essential functions of the educated Europeans in the progress of the country. By stating, again and again, the false doctrine that there would never be any real wealth, prosperity, or progress for the African, so long as the wicked foreigners remained, the leaders, in the end, managed to persuade a great many that this was the truth. For them it was essential that this idea should be believed, because, until it was accepted by a high proportion of their followers, the rest of the programme could not be carried into effect.

In consequence, we find that in the speeches of the leaders designed to further these aims Europeans were constantly being described as the 'people who decimated the Red Indians in America', or 'the people who wiped out the natives of Australia'. It was repeatedly stated by Mau Mau leaders that they knew for certain that the ultimate aim of the Europeans in Kenya was to exterminate the Kikuyu.

When these various aims of Mau Mau are looked at critically, one marvels that well-educated Africans (and there were not a few among the Mau Mau leaders) could ever have used such fallacious arguments. They certainly were well aware that they were not true, but a callous disregard of truth is one of the fundamental weapons of the leaders of this type of political movement.

It would be wrong to imagine that because the main theme, underlying the aims of the movement, was directed against the Europeans, that the other main foreign element in the country—the Asian community—was to be welcomed. The dislike of the Asian was never stressed in Mau Mau propaganda, but, within Mau Mau circles, it was always understood that while the first object was to destroy European power in Kenya, once that was achieved, the problem of driving out the Asians would be easy. It was a matter of policy to enlist (as a temporary measure) as much sympathy as possible among the Asians. Mau Mau top circles have always frowned upon acts of violence against that community, as being contrary to the immediate aims and likely to hinder the achievement of the first stage—the removal of Europeans—to be followed only in a later stage by a similar treatment of the Asians.

6. *Abolish soil conservation*

The sixth aim of Mau Mau is to 'abolish soil conservation'. This seems at first sight a very extraordinary aim for a movement which places so much emphasis on land, since the whole object of the soil conservation measures which Government enforces is to safeguard the land and improve it for agriculture.

To understand the motive of the aim, it is essential to remember that the movement aimed at arousing the sympathy of all members of the tribe, of *both sexes*. In Kikuyu country the greater part of the cultivation of the soil is done by women, who are, on the whole, very conservative in their methods.

Ever since Government introduced its soil conservation programme—with its digging of contour trenches, the planting of wash stops and grass leys—the women of the tribe have been in bitter opposition. To them, time spent on work of this sort was so much less time available for cultivation (as they understood it). Moroever, the schemes decreased the area available for cultivation (while at the same time improving the soil and actually increasing output).

Since most of the *other* aims of Mau Mau had little appeal

to the women of the tribe, this one of 'abolish soil conservation' was introduced with the express aim of winning widespread support from the women of the tribe.

7. *Increase secular education*

This seventh and final aim of Mau Mau also seems somewhat paradoxical in view of the fact that Mau Mau has been consistently burning down schools and killing school teachers. Actually the attacks upon schools and upon school teachers are not a *paradox*; for the schools attacked and teachers killed are those of Government and the missions.

Mau Mau included this aim in order to attract to itself the vast numbers of the youth of the country, who are always clamouring for more and yet more educational facilities. At the same time Mau Mau is not willing that they should acquire their education through Government and mission channels, where there would be less chance to inculcate their own political doctrines.

Mau Mau leaders, however, have always claimed that, should they win the fight, they will provide *compulsory education* for all the young people of the tribe and greatly extend secondary school facilities. In this way they hoped to lure the youth of the country to their cause.

III

MAU MAU ORGANISATION

At the time when I completed my earlier book there was still a great deal that was not known about how Mau Mau was organised, while, of course, as the conflict has grown many changes in Mau Mau organisation have taken place, as the leaders have introduced modifications of original plans to suit the changing needs.

In my first book I made it quite clear that for the majority of Kikuyu, Mau Mau was synonymous with K.A.U., or the Kenya African Union, and was, moreover, nothing more than an extension of the old 'Kikuyu Central Association', under a new guise and with some modifications.

It has since been established and proved in the courts of the country that the Kenya African Union during 1951–2 was being used, at least in Kikuyu country, as a cover for Mau Mau propaganda and activities. Huge meetings of the Union were convened and held all over the Kikuyu Reserve, in Nairobi and wherever else there were Kikuyu, as, for example, in the European settled areas. These meetings were open to the public and were frequently attended by Police representatives. Consequently the speakers took good care that their speeches were just outside the range of what could be called subversive. Nevertheless they often included much that was very near the border-line, and statements about land which were both untrue and calculated to create unrest in the minds of the hearers were commonly made. Before many of these meetings started, the so-called 'New Hymns' were sung, under the excuse that it was necessary to entertain the crowds while waiting for the speakers to appear. But these 'new hymns', set to the tunes of well-known Christian hymns, were in fact nothing but very clever propaganda to prepare the minds of the people for Mau Mau. This we shall discuss further in another chapter.

When the big public meetings were over, smaller groups would meet for real Mau Mau meetings and for oath administration ceremonies. Not unnaturally, people who had listened to the 'hymns' and perhaps joined in singing them and who had heard speeches calculated to instil hatred and distrust of the White Man, were the more ready, a few hours later, to be told about how plans were being made to drive out the White Man and how they could help by taking the oath and joining the movement.

The Kenya African Union, as such, had to remain *on the surface* a genuine inter-tribal political body aiming to provide a means whereby Africans could bring to notice their genuine grievances. If it had failed to do so, it would have invited Government suspicion. Consequently a number of non-Kikuyu were selected to be on the Executive Committee, and branches were formed among other tribes, which, in the main, retained their true character and were not a cover for Mau Mau. But even these branches among other tribes were not wholly free from the taint of Mau Mau, since leading Kikuyu K.A.U. office bearers would occasionally go and address meetings at such branches and make speeches which were calculated to cause unrest. These they would follow up with private talks that aimed to win non-Kikuyu to the Mau Mau cause.

It is doubtful whether the full Executive Committee of K.A.U. was ever used as a part of the Mau Mau organisation, but a high proportion of the individual members of the Executive were, nevertheless, also the top executives of Mau Mau itself. It was thus possible to hold Mau Mau executive meetings and, if a query was raised, to say it was a K.A.U. meeting.

Below the top executive level, Mau Mau was, in the

main, organised along traditional Kikuyu lines with suitable modifications, where necessary, in view of modern trends. In the Native Land Unit, or Kikuyu Reserve, the three Kikuyu districts of Kiambu, Fort Hall, and Nyeri each had a District Executive Committee which was responsible for the whole district and which was represented on the Central Council. Under each District Council were lesser councils on the old *Rugongo* system and beneath these there were 'cells' at the *Mwaki* and *Itura*[1] levels.

Outside the Native Land Unit there had to be some modification of this Kikuyu system, and so in places like Nairobi, where there was a vast Kikuyu population drawn from all the different Kikuyu districts, there were set up three main town Councils, representing the three Kikuyu districts. Each of these had its own subsidiary Council at lower levels in each and every one of the Native Locations in the City. These lower councils roughly corresponded to the *Rugongo* councils in the Reserves, and were split into cells at an even lower level.

In order to provide good cover for its meetings, Mau Mau made extensive use of all kinds of subsidiary organisations that existed ostensibly for purely social purposes: organisations like the Kikuyu General Union, the Kikuyu Club, the Kikuyu Musical Society, and so on. These organisations held very frequent tea parties, dances, and sing-songs at which the new 'hymns' were sung. Under cover of these social occasions opportunity was provided for local meetings of Mau Mau groups, as well as for oath ceremonies later in the evening.

The main functions of the Councils at different levels were (i) the passing on of orders and instructions from the top level, (ii) the enrolment of new members and the

[1] A Rugongo, literally a ridge, was a large administrative unit in olden days. Each Rugongo was divided into a number of Mwaki, and each Mwaki into a number of Itura. Details will be found in my book, *Mau Mau and the Kikuyu*, pp. 34–5.

administration to them of the oath, (*iii*) the collection of funds, (*iv*) the spread of propaganda, and (*v*) the collection of information about Kikuyu who were opposed to the movement.

Each Council, at every level was, in theory at least, composed of nine principal members consisting of Chairman and Vice-Chairman, Secretary and Assistant Secretary, Treasurer and Assistant Treasurer, and three ordinary members. Each member, from Chairman downwards, normally had a deputy, usually (probably always) chosen by himself. These deputies attended meetings and in the absence of the person for whom they were deputy, took his place and carried on for him. The great strength of this system was that it provided for continuity and if a member died, or was arrested, or was absent for any other cause, the group was not disrupted. That is one of the reasons why the mere arrest and detention of some 130 principal leaders, on the declaration of the State of Emergency in October 1952, had such relatively little crippling effect on the movement. The deputies of the persons concerned were automatically ready and able to take over the duties of those arrested, and to carry on.

Sometimes the people selected as oath administrators were also actually members of an organising group—in some other capacity—but more often they were not, but simply maintained close contact with the group. Every Council and each level appointed its own 'Askaris' or police, whose duties were very variable. They included acting as sentries, to see that meetings were not surprised by the authorities; being present at oath ceremonies to administer physical punishment to persons who were reluctant to take the oath and to murder those who utterly refused to do so; to act as messengers between one group and another, and also to serve as intelligence agents.

These 'Askaris' were always armed: with a knife or a sword, or where possible with fire-arms, and from their ranks were drawn the gunmen whose duty it was to go out to seek and shoot loyalists, when instructed to do so.

Many of these 'Askaris' were recruited from the ranks of the criminal classes, 'jail-birds' who, in return for performing these duties, were assured of very considerable protection in any crimes that they committed. Under the terms of the Mau Mau oath no Kikuyu who had taken it could report any other member to the police, even if he himself had been the victim of such a crime as the theft of his bicycle, or of money, or had been brutally beaten up.

Linked with the Councils, at the different levels, there were Mau Mau 'Courts of Justice', roughly corresponding to Police Courts, Magistrates Courts, and the Supreme Court. In most cases a proportion of the 'Court' officials were the same people who were also members of the Councils. The 'Courts' at the lower levels were only allowed to deal with minor offences among the members of their own group, inflicting fines and other penalties for breaking minor rules. If the lower 'Courts' thought that more severe sentences were required, they had to pass on their prisoners to the 'Courts' linked to the Councils of the higher levels, who could, and frequently did, condemn the victims to death.

If this happened, the duty of carrying out the execution fell upon the so-called 'Askaris', but any ordinary member of the group could be called upon to help dispose of the corpse, secretly, and if he refused to do so, would find himself before the 'Court', with a charge which would render him in his turn liable to the death penalty.

In the beginning each group was ordered to do all it could to obtain supplies of arms and ammunition and to keep these in readiness for when they would be required. Thus the collection of these things by theft and robbery was initiated. Certain persons, at various levels, were made responsible for the safe-keeping and control of arms and ammunition, but they seldom had any part in obtaining them in the first place.

The declaration of the State of Emergency took Mau Mau by surprise, for they were certainly not then ready for acts of violence on a big scale. Immediately, therefore, there was a very marked movement by selected people into the forests of the Aberdares, and of Mount Kenya, for training as an army. Suitable people were next selected for different types of leadership, while a major recruiting campaign was initiated, as well as a very increased drive to secure more arms and ammunition.

Those who formed the army kept in constant touch with the various Councils of the higher levels and through them the supply of weapons, clothing, blankets, food, and medical stores was duly organised. Couriers regularly came to Nairobi with messages and returned with the things needed by the forest gangs.

In view of the risk of written messages being intercepted by security forces, documentary methods were only seldom used and, when they were, they were nearly always so worded as to be seemingly innocuous.

To this end Mau Mau developed a most complex system of every-day words to indicate things other than they seemed to mean and these 'code words' were frequently changed. Examples of these 'code words' are 'Makara' which normally means charcoal, for ammunition; 'Muti' which normally means a tree, for a gun; 'Kamwaki' which means a little fire, for a revolver or pistol; and 'Kihii' which means an overgrown boy, for a gunman.

Not only was a constant communication system maintained between the 'army' in the forests and the various Councils at upper level in Nairobi and elsewhere that were responsible for collecting food, supplies, etc., but an organisation was also set up—mainly with women as couriers—to make and maintain contact with detained leaders in detention camps.

In Nairobi itself there was set up a carefully planned system for recruiting men to join the 'army' in the forests and for sending them forward in groups. After the initial few months no Mau Mau member was allowed to go off and join the forest gangs on his own initiative. He had to pass instead through the recruiting organisation so that his bona fides could be carefully checked.

The value of a good intelligence system has always been appreciated by the Kikuyu ever since the days of the ancestral wars with the Masai and the Mau Mau organised a system of getting their own followers into key positions where they could find out what was happening and report to their leaders. Chosen men obtained positions as house-boys and chauffeurs in the households where there was the greatest likelihood of being able to learn things about the plans of Security Forces. Others were encouraged to get jobs in Government Offices, in the Police, and in the Home Guards and the Telephone Service. Since the Kikuyu have always supplied a variable proportion of the employees of these categories in normal times and since there are many genuinely loyal Kikuyu still in such jobs, it was and still is very difficult indeed to distinguish between the spy and the genuine loyalist.

Moreover, by no means all those employed on such intelligence work were drawn from the ranks of the Kikuyu. Enough members of other tribes had been won over to the Mau Mau cause to make it possible to use members of these other tribes in this intelligence organisation.

It was not long before Mau Mau realised that the various special systems of passes and identity cards and 'history of employment' cards with photographs could be usefully turned to their own benefit instead of to their disadvantage. A special organisation was therefore created, within the movement, to supply forged papers which would enable gunmen and gangsters to pass muster as genuine employees of reputable firms if they were picked up during a screening operation.

Long before the State of Emergency was declared those who were engaged in organising the Mau Mau movement realised to the full that they could do a very great deal for their cause by influencing young Kikuyu in schools.

In 1929 there had been a breakaway by a large body of Kikuyu from the established Christian Missions and the organisation of two Kikuyu Church and School organisations known as the Kikuyu African Orthodox Church and the Kikuyu Pentecostal Church, each with its own secular school organisation known as the Kikuyu Karingi Schools Association and the Independent Schools Association respectively.

I discussed these organisations in my earlier book and pointed out how closely they were linked with the former Kikuyu Central Association and that some of the schools had already had to be closed down by Government at the time when I was then writing, because of their Mau Mau activities. It is now clear that after Mau Mau really began to get fully organised, it made it a part of its policy to get complete control of the school committees of as many of these Independent Schools and Churches as it could do.

Such schools and churches were then brought within the Mau Mau organisation, both for the purpose of spreading Mau Mau propaganda, as well as for the holding of meetings and the carrying out of oath ceremonies under cover of more regular school activities. And since African schoolboys and schoolgirls tend, in the present state of things in Kenya, to listen more attentively to the views of their educated teachers than those of their less literate or illiterate parents, it was not difficult for this part of the organisation of Mau Mau, once it got going, to inculcate Mau Mau ideas into thousands of youths and girls who were shortly to go out into the world as adults, and to enlist them as active Mau Mauists.

39

The use of the Independent Churches in the spread of Mau Mau doctrines could only be achieved if leading pastors of these Churches were persuaded to join the movement. Every possible effort was therefore made to induce these people not merely to take the Mau Mau oath, but also to become active and not merely passive members of Mau Mau.

Knowing full well that the Kikuyu are basically a religious people, and that there were tens of thousands who had ceased to believe in the religion of their forefathers, but who had also not become genuine churchmen, Mau Mau leaders decided *as part of the organisation of the movement* to give it a 'religious' trend; to set up a religion which was a very strange blend of pseudo-Christianity and utter paganism. This will be discussed more fully in the next chapter.

'Hymns', the words of which were purely political, but set to well-known Christian hymn tunes, were published in large numbers and also special forms of prayer and even a distorted Mau Mau version of the Apostles' Creed.

If these 'hymns', prayers, and creed were to be widely made use of it was vital to win the support of the clergy of the so-called Independent Churches and as far as possible, where possible, the Native pastors of the Mission Churches too.

In respect of the former, this aim was very largely achieved, but in respect of Kikuyu clergy attached to the Missions, a much smaller measure of success was obtained. It nevertheless became possible to establish a religious side to the Mau Mau organisation which gave it a very strong appeal to a certain type of Kikuyu.

The extreme cleverness of the Mau Mau organisers in thus giving a religious twist to their organisation will be more fully appreciated after the next two chapters have been read.

IV

THE MAU MAU RELIGION

Two years ago I stressed that Mau Mau was nothing more than a new expression of the old Kikuyu Central Association; a political body that was banned in 1941 because it had become wholly subversive.

I also stated that, so far as the Kikuyu tribe was concerned, Mau Mau was synonymous with the new body called the Kenya African Union, which has since also been banned.

What I did not realise then, and in fact have only come to appreciate fully in the past few months, was that Mau Mau, while to some extent synonymous with these political organisations, *was in fact a religion and that it owed its successes to this fact more than to anything else at all.*

During the trial of Jomo Kenyatta, the former General Secretary of the Kikuyu Central Association and President of the Kenya African Union, evidence was given by three office bearers of a small branch of the Kenya African Union, that when they had opposed Mau Mau in their branch of K.A.U. in the days before the State of Emergency had been declared, they had been summoned to the Kenya African Union headquarters in Nairobi and told *in so many words* not to worry about Mau Mau or to fight against it because 'Mau Mau is a religion'.

During the course of the trial too, evidence was produced of one single occasion when Mau Mau had been referred to, in one of the new newspapers that supported K.A.U., as 'the religion of Mau Mau'.

Much other evidence was also given pointing to this simple truth, but I must admit that it was not until very recently that the significance of these parts of the evidence become clear to me.

Again and again I have been puzzled to understand why it was that the former leaders of the K.C.A., who, when they worked purely as a political body, had not succeeded in attracting the support of more than ten or fifteen thousand followers, had now won over more than seventy per cent of the tribe to their cause.

The genuine grievances, which the leaders of Mau Mau were exploiting to their own ends, were identically the same as those that were the chief planks in the old K.C.A. platform. Their aims had not changed substantially and the leaders themselves were the very same people who had been behind the K.C.A. Yet the K.A.U.–Mau Mau combination had succeeded in welding the people together in a way that K.C.A. had failed to do, and I was frankly puzzled.

In the olden days the K.C.A. administered a form of oath to its members, Mau Mau was doing the same, but it was using a ceremony in connection with the oath that was far more likely to impress the minds of the people involved. Knowing the great effect that solemn oath ceremonies have upon the Kikuyu (and the fear which an oath accompanied by a ritual of putting blood to the lips could engender), I felt and openly said that it seemed to me that it was the new form of oath, *as such*, that was the driving power—the new factor in the success of the movement.

In this, however, I now realise that I was only partially correct. Without any doubt the magical ceremonies, attendant upon the administration of the Mau Mau oath, do play an important part, and this will be further discussed in the next chapter, but there is much more to it than that.

What I did not at first realise was, that the Mau Mau oath ceremonies of which one heard so much, really represented a sort of ritual 'Confirmation Service' by which the candidate was formally admitted and declared his belief and faith in the new religion.

I am sure now that it was this new religion, of which the oath ceremony formed only a small part, that was the force which was turning thousands of peace-loving Kikuyu into murderous fanatics.

To understand what has really happened and to reach a fuller appreciation of the situation, it is necessary to turn back to the religious history of the Kikuyu people.

Fifty years ago the Kikuyu were still firm believers in the religion of their forefathers and in a chapter of my earlier book I have given some details of those beliefs, which I need not therefore discuss again here. It was a religion which had very much in common with that of the Old Testament. God, known variously as Ngai, Mwene Nyaga, and Murungu, was the Supreme and only God, a god who delighted in the sacrifice of animals to him at the places of worship, a god whom the individual as well as the priest could pray to.

The coming of European civilisation, with all the superiority of material culture that it brought with it, very soon caused many Kikuyu to begin to turn away from the religion of their fathers and to seek the religion of the white man. Since the white man was superior in so much else, his religion, too, was expected to be superior.

The coming of the Christian Missionaries naturally speeded up this process of turning away from the old to new beliefs and, in the early days, when Christianity was being taught by earnest Missionaries to only a handful of adherents, it was not difficult to lead them into true and sincere Christianity. There were, of course, always a few who did not really believe in Christ's teaching, but many did, and the staunchest opponents of Mau Mau are to be found among those for whom the teachings of Christ were real.

But the swing away from the religion of their fathers was

proceeding very fast, and the number of European Missionaries available to lead and guide the Kikuyu into Christianity were too few. As time went on, more and more of the training had to be done at massed classes for religious instruction and by sermons, and no longer by individual contact between the Missionary and the disciple.

The time came when even the classes in religious instruction could not all be given by the European Missionary himself, and African pastors and teachers, many of them very sincere indeed, had to play their part in training the people who were seeking baptism.

In time the question of whether a candidate for baptism should be baptised came, very often, to depend upon a brief interview, when his knowledge of what he had learnt in the religious classes was tested, and an attempt (sincere, but not always successful) was made to assess whether or not he really wanted to follow Christ and understood what this meant.

And so, gradually, over the years, there grew up a very large number of Kikuyu men and women who were nominally Christian, who had been baptised and perhaps also confirmed, but for whom Christianity was really little more than an outer cloak.

To make matters worse, the time came when the infant children of Kikuyu Christian parents (often themselves only nominally Christian) were received for infant baptism and became the bearers of an outward sign of Christianity, a christian name. But there was no guarantee that they would grow up as anything more than nominal Christians, and many of them did not.

The position was aggravated still further by the fact that, for very many years, almost the whole of the elementary secular education for the Kikuyu (and other tribes) was left solely in the hands of the Mission Schools. At first sight, this was not a bad thing. It meant that those who sought to learn to read and write and achieve other forms of book learning, could only do so through attending Mission Schools where they would also get religious instruction.

But there was another and less satisfactory side to that picture. It meant that if a youth wanted the advantages that he hoped would come to him from secular education, he had to *pretend* to be interested in the Christian religion, had to attend the religious classes and become a candidate for baptism, even if all the time he had no real use for Christianity at all.

Thousands thus combined attendance at secular Mission Schools with temporary membership of the Mission Church organisation, only to abandon all thoughts of Christian teaching the moment their secular education was completed.

Another major factor also played a big part in the growth of a huge body of men and women who were no longer believers in the religion of their forefathers, but who also had no real Christian faith. This factor was the failure of most Missionaries (and also of supporters of the Missionary Society and leaders in the Mother Country) to realise that there was a vast difference between the simple teachings of Christ himself, the religion of the New Testament, and what passed in the twentieth century as Christianity. So much that was not fundamental to a simple belief in Christ and his teaching had been added. Some of it was nothing more than western social custom, some was due to the assimilation into Christianity of the teaching of the 'Early Fathers'.

Moreover, different Christian Missions, according to the sect to which they belonged, presented different versions of twentieth-century Christianity, when what was needed was a simple transition from Old Testament religion (which was so like the Kikuyu old beliefs) to that of the New Testament and Christ Himself.

The Bible had been translated into Kikuyu and could be read by all who had achieved a measure of secular education. The heroes of the Old Testament had more

45

than one wife, but they were still praised and held in deep respect by the Christian Church. Nowhere in the New Testament could the Kikuyu find any word from Christ Himself condemning the polygamy of the Old Testament, or saying that if a man had more than one wife he could not enter the Kingdom of Heaven. Why then did the Missionaries lay such stress upon this? Why were polygamists denied baptism and communion, however sincerely they believed in Christ and His own teaching?

For the Kikuyu polygamy was normal, and the numerical excess of women over men, together with the lack of any outlet for unmarried women to earn an honest living for themselves, made polygamy a necessity.

Many sincere African Christians felt that the Churches were going beyond the teachings of Christ, and they revolted. At first they did not turn against Christianity, they still sincerely believed in Him, and prayed to Him and sought His guidance in their lives, but in the Mission parlance they were 'Back sliders' because they had taken a second wife into a Christian home, 'Back sliders' even if they still believed; still held sincere family worship for themselves, their two wives, and their children; still were trying to live up to His standards.

In vain did some of the older African Christians point out that St. Paul had said that priests and deacons were to be the husband of one wife and that this implied (to them at any rate) that ordinary members of the congregation were not blamed for a plurality of wives.

Those who broke with the Churches on this issue gradually, in most cases, broke altogether from Christianity. That was the tragedy. Since the Missionaries were firm in their view that their particular sect's interpretation of the Gospel was the only right one and that the *Church rules* must be obeyed, in addition to what the New Testament appeared to say, this Christianity was not for them.

The setting up of numerous independent Separatist

46

African Churches was thus an inevitable consequence. The founders of these churches were mostly quite sincere and if their *Church rules* differed from those of the various missions, they nevertheless, *to start with*, were Christian Churches. They were not helped, however, by leaders of the Mission Churches, they were cold-shouldered.

The leaders of the K.C.A. political movement realised that if they could set up a religion which would fulfil the need for a faith, and fill the vacuum, they could achieve much that they had never achieved before.

People, once they have a faith, will fight for that faith and die for it. The whole of history gives us proof of this.

And so the religion of Mau Mau was born.

Since the vast majority of those who were to be won over to Mau Mau were people who already knew the outward forms of the Christian religion, and who knew nothing of the forms of worship of fifty years before, Mau Mau had to be largely based (in its presentation) upon Christianity. A creed was drawn up, based upon the Apostles' Creed, but altered to a hideous parody of it. It was printed and circulated widely and on the cover of the printed form was an exhortation to all who considered themselves to be 'true children of Mumbi and Gikuyu' (the Eve and Adam of the tribe) to learn this creed by heart, to say it every morning and evening and to have faith in it. It was a creed affirming faith in Almighty God, but also in His supposedly chosen leaders of the tribe, the leaders of Mau Mau, with Jomo Kenyatta taking the place of Jesus Christ.

Many of the preachers and leaders of the Independent Separatist Churches were won over to the K.C.A. political cause, and, by easy stages, to Mau Mau as a religion. Then they preached sermons and prayed prayers that warned the people that the European religion, while it accepted Almighty God, tried to add to it belief in a false leader, Christ, and not in the leadership of the Kikuyu

47

themselves. They also started to preach that any of the old Kikuyu customs that were allowed by the Bible (whether in the Old Testament or New) were good, and that the Mission Churches had their own hidden reasons for trying to depart from the teaching of the Bible and for condemning polygamy and blood sacrifices and other things which were part of the Kikuyu's ancient beliefs. The religion of Mau Mau was the true religion, and God would bless those who believed in it. Those who opposed it were the opponents of truth and justice and must be fought and resisted by every possible means.

One of the most popular accompaniments of Christianity, as taught by the Missions, was the singing of hymns. Community singing, especially of the more emotional hymns, had a very great appeal to the Kikuyu. Mau Mau religion therefore made use of this form of appeal to the mind and heart of the people.

The people knew and liked the tunes of our Ancient and Modern Hymn Book and the Church Hymnal, but the words were not suited to Mau Mau religion at all. And so new words were written, sometimes mere parodies of the existing translations of Christian hymns, sometimes wholly new ones and the 'Hymn Books of Mumbi and Kikuyu' appeared in print and were at once widely circulated and the hymns sung over and over again.

We shall see in the next chapter that the Mau Mau leaders used these 'hymns' in part to stir up emotion and a belief in God and His chosen leaders and, in part, as very clever propaganda and incitement to murder and arson and brutality.

Once the idea of Mau Mau as a religion had been established, with the leader Kenyatta featuring as the apostle chosen by God, to bring freedom and all good things to his people, it was not difficult to extend the idea further. The Mau Mau oath ceremonies started off as nothing more than what they appeared to be, the swearing-in

of members to follow the rules of the organisation loyally
and never to disobey or to reveal the secrets to unauthorised
persons. The ceremony was then at first a 'swearing-in' in
the ordinary sense of the word.

But it was soon realised that it could be made into
something much more than this. For the ordinary Kikuyu
in the olden days the most solemn period of his life was that
which culminated in initiation into adult status. The
initiation ceremonies of the Kikuyu were always accompanied by acts of a religious nature and linked with the
worship of the supreme God.

No Kikuyu, in the olden days, really became a full
member of the tribe, enjoying the responsibilities, as well
as the benefits, of adult membership of the community,
until he, or she, had been through the initiation ceremonies.

At an early period in the story of the development of the
Mau Mau oath, from the much simpler oath ceremony
of the old and purely political K.C.A., it was made known
that, in future, so far as the leaders of Mau Mau religion
were concerned, no person would be entitled to count as a
true Kikuyu—'a true member of the house of Mumbi and
Gikuyu'—unless he had been 'initiated' by the 'new
initiation ceremony'.

The words for taking an oath are 'Kunyua Muma, and
although the Mau Mau oath was still *sometimes* referred to in
this way, it was increasingly referred to as 'Kurua', 'to be
initiated', using this word because of its most solemn
associations in the minds of all Kikuyu.

No matter whether you had been initiated in the old
sense of the word 'Kurua' before; no matter how much
you had given money to the movement, sung its 'hymns',
joined in its prayers, repeated its creed, you still did not
really belong to 'Mumbi and Gikuyu', you could not
claim the privileges that were coming, unless you 'rua-ed'
in the new sense.

It became customary to open an oath ceremony by

49

solemn prayers to Almighty God, and whenever possible these prayers were conducted by one of the 'priests' of the Independent Churches, wearing his dog collar and even sometimes his vestments, which resemble those of the Church of England.

The prayers were only to Almighty God, addressed sometimes as 'Mwathani Ngai' (the form of address used by the Missionaries), and sometimes as 'Mwene Nyaga', as in the old-time Kikuyu prayers; they asked for blessings on the 'initiation' that was to follow and upon all that was about to be done in God's name.

The oath ceremony itself then followed and, apart from the fact that the persons being sworn in did so in the name of Almighty God, the next stages had nothing whatever in common with any form of Christian worship, except in rare cases of variation.

Occasionally, for example, the people taking the oath were marked with a cross upon their foreheads in imitation of baptism, but it was a cross made in blood.

When every one had duly taken the oath (or, having refused, had been strangled and disposed of), there was usually a short 'sermon' followed by further prayers, to impress upon those present the religious aspect of what they had just been doing.

When a witness at the trial of Jomo Kenyatta gave evidence that a priest (not a pagan priest but a 'Reverend') had been among those officiating at the ceremony, Defence Counsel asked in a clearly disbelieving voice, 'Do you really want the Court to believe that Rev. so and so was helping at this administration of the Mau Mau oath?' the witness answered, 'Yes, it is the truth'. I myself failed to see the full significance, merely thinking, at that time, that this particular priest happened to be a Mau Mau adherent, and was perhaps accidentally present. Now I know that he was there for a set purpose; to give the proceedings their religious twist.

Once Mau Mau was firmly established as a religion, it was very much easier to persuade the followers of the movement that if they had to kill they would be doing so for God and in a righteous cause.

The new teaching said that the followers of Christ were evil people who had been led away from the true God 'Mwene Nyaga' or 'Murungu', led away, even, from God under the name of 'Mwathani Ngai' by lying and deceitful Missionaries. The Christians were made out to be enemies of true religion and, as such, must be treated without mercy.

If a person demanded to know in advance just what was involved in this new ceremony of initiation he was not told. Secrecy about the details of even the simplest 'First Oath' ceremony was strictly maintained within the movement. It was generally known that it involved taking an oath and doing certain solemn things, but that was all. Thus very many, who had become intrigued by the 'hymn' singing, and by the creed of Mau Mauism, asked for full membership, asked to be allowed to 'rua' in the new sense, little knowing what this step was leading them into, except that it was in the cause of Kikuyu freedom.

Others, of course, who never volunteered could be got into the movement by trickery, by threats and by force. It was never expected that those who joined in this way would be very ardent members, but at least it was hoped that they would cease to oppose the movement too openly.

To make the oath ceremony carry the greatest possible weight, and have a big psychological impression upon those who thus 'rua-ed', it was evolved as a strange combination of ideas drawn from Christianity and from the customs of long ago, without attempting to comply exactly with the requirement of either.

In the past (not once but many times), bloody deeds and horrible cruelties have been perpetrated in the name of God and religion by peoples with a much longer background of 'civilisation' than the Kikuyu, and it is this driving force which more than anything else has made Mau Mau what it is.

When to this religious aspect of the movement the great power exercised by the magical and mystical acts that accompany the actual oath-taking are added, it is not so difficult to see how it became possible to make so many normally peace-loving Kikuyu into the fanatical, murdering maniacs that they have become under Mau Mau.

MAU MAU PROPAGANDA

As I have already indicated, both in my earlier book and
in the preceding chapters, the Kenya African Union, which
started as a constitutional organisation pledged to provide
a platform for the airing of genuine grievances and for seeking to persuade the Government to right genuine wrongs
through constitutional channels, gradually, for the majority
of the Kikuyu tribe, became a cover for Mau Mau activities.
In fact, in about 1951, K.A.U. and Mau Mau became
synonymous. Branches of K.A.U. whose local leaders
were opposed to Mau Mau were either closed down, or
the office bearers were dismissed and replaced by others
who were willing to toe the line.

If, therefore, we want to study Mau Mau propaganda
methods in the period leading up to the declaration of the
State of Emergency in October 1952, it is the K.A.U. propaganda machine (in so far as it was directed towards the
Kikuyu) that we want to examine. Mau Mau as such and
the K.C.A. published nothing, for they were banned, and
if they did so would at once attract attention to their
underground activity.

The leaders of the Mau Mau movement, who were
operating under cover of K.A.U., were quick to realise
the very great opportunity which the Kikuyu love of hymn
singing offered for propaganda purposes. In the first place
propaganda in 'hymn' form and set to well-known tunes
would be speedily learned by heart and sung over again
and again and thus provide a most effective method of
spreading the new ideas. The fact that such 'hymns' would
be learned by heart, by those who could read them, and
then taught to others, meant that they would soon also

become well known to the illiterate members of the tribe. This was very important, for there were many who could not be reached by ordinary printed propaganda methods.

More important still, these propaganda messages could safely be sung in the presence of all but a very few Europeans, since the vast majority could not understand a word of Kikuyu and if they heard a large, or a small, group singing to the tune of 'Onward Christian Soldiers', 'Abide with Me', or any other well-known hymn, they were hardly likely to suspect that propaganda against themselves was going on under their very noses. They would be more likely to consider that a Christian revival was on its way.

The Kikuyu leaders of K.A.U. who were also running Mau Mau were most anxious to achieve three things: (i) to enlist as many Kikuyu as possible as members of K.A.U. and, through it, of Mau Mau; (ii) to prepare the minds of all Kikuyu for the day when Mau Mau would drive out the White Man and kill off all those Kikuyu who supported them; (iii) to ensure that no hint of the real link between K.A.U. and Mau Mau should leak out to those in authority.

The 'hymns', therefore, could and did contain frequent references to K.A.U. (on the face of it, a recognised peace-loving, constitutional body) and could openly appeal to all to join the body. At the same time, in order to achieve the second object, the 'hymns' must work up a deep hatred for the White Man and for the loyalists and must prepare the ground for violence. But since K.A.U. was ostensibly a peace-loving body pledged to use nothing but constitutional methods, the 'hymn-books' must in no circumstances be officially linked with K.A.U. If it should become necessary, it must be possible for K.A.U. leaders to deny all knowledge of the books and so keep the African Union in the clear. If any question were ever raised the leaders must be able to say that over-zealous followers had acted without their knowledge in writing and printing these 'hymn-books'.

The 'hymn-books', therefore, while calling on people to join K.A.U. and extolling by name those K.A.U. Kikuyu leaders who were also the planners of Mau Mau, never appeared as official K.A.U. publications. Many of them were, however, distributed through K.A.U. head office and its branches, and the 'hymns' were regularly sung at K.A.U. meetings. In fact, to the masses, these books were known as 'K.A.U. Hymn Books'.

The first of these so-called 'hymn-books' to appear in print was probably that compiled and edited by Kinuthia Mugia.[1] It is undated, but neither in the introduction nor in the preface is there any reference to other similar 'hymn-books', whereas the prefaces of later books all refer to 'earlier hymn-books' that have appeared. The introduction to the book was written by the then editor of a Kikuyu newspaper called *Mumenyereri*. This preface is, I think, worth translating in full before I give translations of some of the actual 'hymns', since it is very revealing. It reads:

'I am one of those who persuaded Mr. Kinuthia Mugia, the singer of these hymns[2] to have them printed in book form. I have to admit that when I first heard some of them sung by him I felt a mixture of sorrow and joy in my heart, until my tears flowed, whether I liked it or not. When, therefore, he says in his preface that "hymns are a voice which penetrates quickly to the heart" I wholly support this opinion of his.

'These hymns of his are connected with things that are taking place at the present time and when, therefore, they are sung at meetings[3] they enter the hearts of the people gathered together, in an excellent way, and form, as it were, a foundation for the speeches of the leaders.

[1] Kinuthia Mugia is detained under the Emergency Regulation as a leading Mau Mau organiser.
[2] Before they were printed he used to go about singing them rather like a bard in olden days.
[3] They were regularly sung at K.A.U. meetings in Kikuyu country before the speakers arrived.

'Another thing which Mr. Kinuthia has done, which is most valuable, is to write down some real Kikuyu hymns such as have been known to the Kikuyu from the beginning. Of these one is the one called "Kaari" which used to be sung by the warriors when they had conquered in battle, while another is the hymn of the cultivators which used to be sung to a lazy person in order to make him zealous in his work.

'Therefore Mr. Kinuthia should be thanked by all Kikuyu people for having consented to have these hymns printed, so that they may reach all the many people now living, as well as those who will come after us, for as Gikuyu[1] said "the spoken word is never lost".'

The following extracts from Mr. Kinuthia's own preface to the 'hymns' will also be of interest before we turn to the hymns themselves:

'Hymns form a voice which reaches speedily not only the ears but also the very hearts of the people and if you think over this statement quietly you will realise how true it is.

'Hymns are prayers which reach God quickly.

'These hymns are a gift sent by God and revealed through one person and since an apostle is sent unto the masses, are you not one of the masses?'

We thus see that the method of propaganda via 'hymns' was especially chosen because it was a quick and effective way to reach the hearts of the people and to prepare them to receive the speeches and ideas of their leaders. The 'hymns' were, moreover, specifically announced as being the result of a special revelation by God and were thereby given the blessing and force of supernatural messages.

Since it would occupy too much space in this book to translate all Mr. Kinuthia's thirty-eight 'hymns', I shall have to be content with giving enough extracts to indicate the nature of the propaganda which they contain.

[1] The traditional Adam, joint founder of the tribe with Mumbi.

The first hymn[1] is by way of being a hymn of welcome, to be sung to those who have assembled at a K.A.U. meeting and it is immediately followed by No. 2 which consists of the most fulsome praise of Jomo Kenyatta. The hymn reads as follows:

'God makes his covenant shine until it is brighter than the sun, so that neither hill nor darkness can prevent him coming to fulfil it, for God is known as the Conqueror.

'He told Kenyatta in a vision "You shall multiply as the stars of heaven, nations will be blessed because of you". And Kenyatta believed him and God swore to it by his mighty power.

'Kenyatta will find happiness before God, for he is the foundation stone of the Kingdom. He has patiently suffered pain in his heart, he is moreover the Judge of the Kikuyu, and will dispense justice over the House of Mumbi.[2]

'Kenyatta is the foundation stone of the Kingdom, his house shall never lack a light, nor will it ever lack a centre pole, provided for him by the God of the Kikuyu, namely justice.

'Kenyatta made a Covenant with the Kikuyu saying he would devote his life to them, and would go to Europe to search for the power to rule, so as to be a judge over the House of Mumbi. I ask myself "Will we ever come out of this state of slavery?"

'He went, he arrived there and he came back. He promised the Kikuyu "When I return M—— shall go in order to arrange for the return of our land". May God have mercy upon us.

'When the day for his[3] return comes he will come with the decisions about our land and the building which he said he would come to erect at Githunguri ya Wairera shall be the one in which our rule shall be established.'

[1] For the rest of this chapter, I shall not put the word hymn in inverted commas, since it is now clear that they are only hymns in a limited sense.
[2] Mumbi is the traditional 'Eve' of the Kikuyu tribe.
[3] i.e. M——'s.

D.M.M.—5   57

The third hymn is in praise of education and calls upon the people to give their support to the Independent Schools, which of course were under Mau Mau control.

The fourth hymn is an attack on those who are alleged not to have the interests of their own peoples at heart, that is to say, those who work for the European interests.

The fifth hymn in the book is a lament for the lost Kikuyu lands, and the sixth a lament over the Kikuyu who were removed from the Olengernone settlement and taken to Yatta. Some comment on this event is necessary, for the alleged injustice over the Olengernone settlement is one of the many events that was selected by Mau Mau leaders as a major weapon to stir up anti-European feelings. Here, therefore, is a summary of what happened there.

A number of Kikuyu families had settled in the neighbourhood of Narok, in Masai-land, over a fairly long period of time and, to some extent, with the consent of the Masai themselves. But as their numbers increased they became somewhat of an embarrassment to the Masai tribe and finally Government, realising that these people had no land of their own to return to in Kikuyu country, offered them very generous settlement terms at a place called Olengernone. One of the very few conditions laid down was that the acreage that each man was granted must be properly farmed and not ruined, while a limit was set to the number of stock any one household could have so as to prevent over-grazing the settlement grasslands.

Once established at Olengernone the Kikuyu settlers proceeded to disregard all the conditions, which they had earlier consented to, and, after repeated warnings, Government finally lost patience and forcibly removed those who had done so.

Naturally, the political agitators never mentioned how the agreed conditions had been flouted, or how patient and forbearing Government had been, before it finally took action. Instead they made use of the eviction of the

Olengernone Kikuyu (from land which had been only given to them on certain conditions) as a major grievance and as evidence of the gross injustice of the White Man.

The ninth hymn is an unconcealed call to violence against those Kikuyu who side with the Europeans. Verses three and four in particular read:

'Let the hypocrites among the tribe remember that the time will come when they will be like "Judas".

'The time has come for all these hypocrites to be burned.'

The word 'Hinga' which is here translated as hypocrite is the one which Mau Mau members normally apply to the loyalists and to African Government Servants.

Verse twelve of hymn 10, which is otherwise mainly a lament, is also significant, it reads:

'The Europeans came from Europe in order to oppress the House of Mumbi. They live here and continually oppress us. Oh, when will they go back to Europe?'

Hymn 18 is entitled 'Oppression' and after praising Jomo Kenyatta as the one person who has pity on his heart for the Kikuyu whose land has been stolen from them, goes on in verse five:

'As for you, you Europeans, know ye well that on the day when God comes to our aid you will be driven out.'

Hymn 19, which was a very popular one indeed, runs as follows:

'God created Gikuyu and Mumbi and placed them in Kikuyu land, but they were deceived by the Europeans and their land was stolen from them.'

Chorus:
'I will never abandon Jomo, he has promised that our land will be returned to us.

59

'K—— stood up at Ringuti and said, "The feckless and the lazy are but common people in the land".

'Sorrow and oppression come with the European, when we believed them we became paupers.

'One thing pleased us, Education was not an evil, now all you children of Mumbi let us unite.

'M—— went to Europe and returned with wisdom for our children, now you children learn and become wise.'

Kenyatta said to those who think only of themselves ('Ereriri' here translated, those who think only of themselves is another popular Mau Mau name for the loyalists who are said to be thinking only of their own pockets, when they side with the White Man).

'Why are you selling out our descendants, don't you realise you will be accursed?'

Hymn 20 is in praise of the building of the so-called Kenya Teachers' College at Githunguri, where teachers were trained for the Independent Schools that were used to spread the Mau Mau doctrine.

Hymn 24 starts off with an account of the visits of Mr. Fenner Brockway to the Kikuyu and goes on in verse eight:

'As for "you who love Europeans",[1] ask yourselves what help they will be to you when you are left alone after having betrayed your people.

'Truly slavery is evil and you are perpetuating slavery.'

The final verse of hymn 25 is a warning to those who are on the side of the White Man. It reads:

'The Europeans are only guests and they will leave this land of ours. Then, you traitors, what will happen to you when the Kikuyu rise up?'

[1] The loyalists.

Hymn 26, after praising Mau Mau leaders by name, contains another warning to the loyalists.

'Let the man who betrays his people, seeking fame for himself, remember the curse that is on him.'

Verse two of hymn 28 reads:

'If only this was the days of old I would seize my spear and sword and go and slay them by Mount Kenya.'

Hymn 31 is very significant and reads:

'We beg you, our parents and our friends, to harken to us, and we will not abuse you.'
Chorus:
'Tell the elders to shut up, they let our lands be taken. Tell the young men to rise up in arms so that our lands may be returned to us.

'When the Europeans came they came with great cunning saying they came to make us wise, but really they came to deceive us.

'The time has come to open our eyes and our ears. Our hearts, too, must be opened.

'The whole land is nothing but darkness and the squatter system, when the young men want to rise up they are told, "The time is not yet".'[1]

I have given only a few translations from this first of the propaganda hymn-books, since it would take up too much space to do otherwise and I must now pass on to the others that soon followed.

Like the first, the next book is undated, but it is rather more definitely linked with the Kenya African Union. It was edited by Muthee Cheche, who is said to have

[1] The elders were always telling the young men that they must not try to rise up and rebel. The hymn-book now tells them to do so and at the same time calls on the elders to 'shut up'.

composed many of the 'hymns' himself and who certainly often sang them. It was on sale through Kiburi House, the headquarters of the Nairobi branch of K.A.U., but at the Kapenguria trial, Jomo Kenyatta, the President of K.A.U., denied that he had any knowledge of this, or had sanctioned it.

Muthee Cheche was detained at a very early date after the State of Emergency was declared, as a prominent Mau Mau leader. There have even been many rumours that Jomo Kenyatta had nominated him as immediate successor should anything happen to himself.

The first hymn in the book to the tune of 'Jesus will come' translates as follows:

'One day the elders of K.A.U. met at Kaloleni[1] and it seemed good to them to go into secret session to plan for the return of the land.'

Chorus:

'Come all you Kikuyu and summon, too, all Mumbi and let us plan secretly now: we are full of sorrow because of our soil which has been taken from us without our consent.

'First, they said, you will observe certain things happening without understanding the reason for them. Secondly they said, "We can hear but your ears are still closed".

'We are overcrowded in our homes and we no longer have good grazing, good cultivation areas have we no longer, but we are always being called upon to dig soil conservation trenches.

'Let every man ask himself, let every one ask himself, "How do I stand with the black races?" for the time is soon coming like the days of long ago when the evil people will be burned.[2]

[1] Kaloleni Hall in Nairobi where many of the meetings of K.A.U. were held.

[2] The time is coming when those who are not on the side of the black people, i.e. those who help the Europeans, will be burnt to death. This has been all too truly fulfilled; many loyalists have been brutally burned alive.

'Jomo Kenyatta, son of man, dedicated himself to agitate about the land of all the black people.

'M—— dedicated himself in respect of education, until such time as another like him could take his place. Let all black children study hard until they are like M——.

'Pray all you who are the sons of black men that M—— may return to us bringing self-government. We shall rejoice all together, we black people, when our land is returned to us.

'You Europeans make merry now, for the day is coming when you will weep, because of the evil you have done. May you be destroyed in the sea.'

Hymn 2 in the book reads:

'There is a great wailing in the land of the black people because of land hunger, you fools and wise people alike, is there any among you who is not aware of the over-crowding in our land.

'You Europeans you are nothing but robbers, though you pretended you came to lead us. Go away, go away you Europeans, the years that are past have been more than enough for us.

'You divided us into police and common people and if the common people failed they were punished, and if a policeman was bribed he too was punished. Go away, go away you Europeans, the years that are past have been more than enough for us.

'You of Kikuyu and Mumbi fight hard, that we may be given self-government, that our land may be given back to us. The corn is ripe for harvest, if we are late the harvest will be lost.

'You who betray the people,[1] I ask myself what will happen to you when the Europeans have gone back to their own land?

'Long ago the Europeans came upon us with weapons of war and they drove us out and took our land. Go

---

[1] Yet another threat to the loyalists.

away, go away you Europeans, the time has come to strangle and —— (the last word is misprinted in the book, and as it stands means nothing at all).'

Hymn 6 in this book is mainly in praise of M——, but verse five reads:

'For those who oppress the people vengeance is now ready; God will send a sword from Mount Kenya.'

Hymn 8 is an open attack on those who work for the Europeans. They are frequently referred to as 'Thaka', the well-dressed, or beautiful, because, through employment by the white man they can afford better things than others. The chorus runs:

'Happy are those who have refused to work for the Europeans, but have instead become agitators for the people.'

Hymn 9 is in praise of Dedan Mugo, son of Kimani, who was tried and convicted of serious Mau Mau offences before the State of Emergency was declared. The hymn tells of his arrest and holds him up as a great hero and martyr.

Hymn 14 is in praise of Kenyatta who has returned and is at Githunguri.[1] Verse three reads:

'What did the Europeans come to find here, they only brought a curse upon us and wiped out our goats.'

Verse four reads:

'Those who now side with the Europeans, in order to curry favour, will never achieve it, but they will soon be very sorry.'

[1] The place where the Government of the Kikuyu was to be established one day.

Hymn 15 is an attack upon the Europeans, the first verse reads:

'Come together and weep. See how the Europeans oppress us and make us submit to thumb-printing.'

The fourth verse reads:

'As for you Europeans, who have so long oppressed us, go.'

Verse five is another threat of violence against the loyalists.

'As for you who side with the Europeans, on the day when God hears us, you will be wiped out.'

Hymn 16 is also an attack upon the Europeans and those Kikuyu who side with them. In this case the whole hymn is worth translating:

'When the Europeans came from Europe they said they came to give us learning and we accepted them gladly, but woe upon us, they really came to oppress us.

'Those who hate the house of Mumbi and say they prefer the Europeans, will have great trouble in Kikuyu land when we achieve self-government.

'When the house of Mumbi meets in order to recruit others to the house of Mumbi[1] there are some who side with the enemy and are like Judas of old.

'You house of Mumbi even if you are oppressed, do not be afraid in your hearts, a Kikuyu proverb says "God help those who help themselves".

[1] This means when members of Mau Mau (who always refer to themselves as the house of Mumbi) meet for an oath ceremony at which others are formally enlisted into the movement, there are some who go and report to the police and take on themselves the role of traitor.

'You who side with the Europeans when they go back to Europe, you will kneel down before us and weep, claiming that you did not realise what you were doing.

'When the Europeans return to Europe you who sell the land of the house of Mumbi we will answer you, by saying, "We disown you even as you disowned us".

'When Kenyatta came back from Europe he came with a spear and sword and shield and a war helmet on his head as a sign for the Kikuyu.

'M—— will return with spear and shield to uplift the house of Mumbi and avenge the oppression which they have suffered from the Europeans.

'Let those who go and report on our doings be accursed by their reports and if they get pay for what they do, let the pay be a curse upon them too.

'Oh, house of Mumbi let us exert ourselves to get our land returned, the land which was ours and stolen from us by the deceitful Europeans.'

Hymn 18 is a hymn in praise of Jomo Kenyatta and an attack upon Europeans and the loyalists who side with them. Verse three reads:

'Those who sell the people to the Europeans are devils, where will they go when we come into our own, they will be wiped out like Sodom.'

Verse six:

'Have no fear in your hearts, God is in heaven. Be brave, God's power is here and the Europeans will be driven out.'

Hymn 22 is set to the tune of 'I think when I read the sweet story of old, of how Jesus died for me'. Instead it tells of how the Europeans have taken the land. The last line of verse two reads:

'Europeans may you go, may you be utterly destroyed.'

Hymn 23 is about how Jomo will bring self-government to the Kikuyu, and how those who choose to side with the White Man will have nowhere to go. With this theme is coupled a call to young men and women to join Kenyatta.

Hymn 24 is a bitter attack on those who side with the Europeans instead of with Jomo Kenyatta, while Hymn 25 also attacks those who side with the Europeans and calls them Judases.

The whole theme of Hymn 26 is that the lands which were stolen by the Europeans will soon be restored.

Hymn 27 is in praise of Jomo and a threat to the Europeans that they will soon have to leave by sea.

Hymn 28 is an attack on Government chiefs and a call to young men to rise up and recover the stolen land.

Hymn 38 is a call to the laggards to join in with the rest of the Kikuyu as *the day is at hand when the land will be given back, and if the laggards do not join the movement now they will not get their share.*

Hymn 39 is an attack on the Europeans and all those who side with them. The Europeans must go and those who side with them are enemies of the tribe. Hymn 40 is a threat to all those who sided with the Europeans, who will be destroyed when the Europeans leave.

By August 1952, the tempo of Mau Mau propaganda was being greatly stepped up. Very little notice had been taken of the earlier hymn-books, as propaganda, and no attempt had been made to ban them. It therefore seemed safe to use this method more openly. Almost simultaneously, on August 15th and 20th 1952 respectively, two new 'hymn-books' were published. In fact they each contained reprints from the earlier books that we have already considered, but in the main their contents were new. Both books were now rather more openly linked with the Kenya African Union, and two hymns appeared in which Jomo Kenyatta is referred to as 'King'. In both cases the English word 'King' is used, because there is no real equivalent to a king in the Kikuyu vocabulary, and they wanted to make it clear that he was to be much more than a mere senior chief or a leading elder.

Still more significant is the fact that both books also contained hymns, *set to the tune of the British National Anthem.* One is a hymn about the land, but the other, under the heading of 'Prayer for the King', says quite openly 'May Kenyatta be victorious'.

In both these new books too, there are hymns which are even more blatant in their threats to 'those who help the Europeans' and to the Christians, who are mockingly called the 'People of the Lamb'.

The following extracts from the hymn-books of 15 August 1952 speak for themselves. Hymn 4 to the tune of 'Here we suffer grief and pain':

'Here we suffer thumb-printing and grass planting. 'T'wont be so when the land is ours.

'The warriors hut is set up, one brave leader is already here, the other is on his way.

'Let the Europeans exert themselves now for the time has come to separate what is theirs and what belongs to others.

'Those who were our friends, but who have become spies will be cast into the sea.

'What is making you hesitate when you hear the call to prepare? You were born to be warriors.

'Their ears are shut, their hearts are shut. Now let us march to war.

'Support your just words with strong deeds that you fall not by the wayside.'

Hymn 5, to the tune of 'Who is He in yonder Stall', consists of a series of questions, which it is left to the singer to answer for himself. Verse three reads:

'Who is he who will weep when Kenyatta is proclaimed King?'

Verse six:

'Who is he who conquers now, conquers the Europeans?
'Who is he who now is ruler over all the country?
'As for you "people of the Lamb", how will you escape?'

Verses three and four of Hymn 8 runs:

'The Europeans have plotted against you of Mumbi
and Kikuyu, but you must all be steadfast like those of
olden times who fought against the Masai and would not
be conquered.

'Even if ten were slain or sixty, still on the morrow
they fought again and would not abandon their objective.'

The twelfth hymn in the book reveals clearly how Mau
Mau was being turned into a pseudo religion with Jomo
Kenyatta as saviour; it runs:

'The Book of the Kikuyu is Holy, it helps me to be
good, it is my guiding principle when I go to join the
Kikuyu.

'The Book is Kenyatta, it is he who leads me, it is he
who saved me by his blood.

'We see the love of Kenyatta in that book. He gave
his life to save us.

'That Book of the Kikuyu will guide me all my life
and make me love M——.

'If I accept the commandments, never again will I be
called "Boy".[1] I will achieve self-government through
Jomo Kenyatta.'

Hymn 19 also has a number of very significant verses;
the whole hymn is worth translating in full:

'Kenyatta will come with a sword for the harvest,
and with a seat for our people when we receive self-
government.

[1] Europeans commonly address their servants as 'Boy', this verse
renounces employment by the White Man.

69

'Because we are true servants of God we shall don the armour of war and tell the Europeans to get out.

'You shall see the house of Mumbi which has so long been oppressed, being granted self-government through Jomo Kenyatta.

'God will save us from those who oppress us and the Europeans will be driven out together with the "Black Europeans".[1]

'Those who have oppressed the people will be thrown into the flames because they were deceived by the Europeans, in order to steal the land.

'They will be asked by the Kikuyu, "Since you sold our land because you were deceived by the Europeans, why do you not follow them now?"

'Happy and blessed is the house of Gikuyu because it has kept faithful to the covenant of the God of Kikuyu.

'We who are Kikuyu will all rejoice when our land, which was sold for the sake of power, is returned to us.'

The last verse of Hymn 23 reads:

'The war will end and we will achieve self-government. Our estates will be returned to us, the estates which were taken from us. Let all of us, of the house of Mumbi, pray that we may conquer the Europeans and get back our land.'

Hymn 25 is a parody of the well-known hymn 'What are you waiting for? Come to Jesus now', only for 'Jesus' K.A.U. is substituted. It contains attacks both upon those who side with the Europeans, and also on all who belong to the established Churches.

Hymn 26 shows very clearly that the aim is to subjugate the Europeans. The fourth verse reads:

'Oh we shall be happy when the Europeans call us "Bwana". At present they call us "Boy" because they don't understand us.

[1] 'The Black Europeans' are the loyalists who, in spite of their black skins, side with the White Man.

'Our good lands were stolen from us and we were cast roughly aside. They forgot that black people have blood like themselves.

'Our M—— will tell us to await him at the aerodrome. It is not money he will bring to us but something that will be of benefit to us for evermore.'

Hymn 28 contains yet another threat to those Kikuyu who are loyal to the Europeans.

'Where will those who side with the White Man sleep? They will spend the rest of their lives as perpetual slaves.

'May God remove these enemies of the black people from among us, let them go back to their homes, we do not want them here.'

Hymn 29 is a spirited call to join K.A.U. The whole hymn is translated since it shows how K.A.U. was openly becoming synonymous with the Mau Mau anti-European movement, although, on paper, it was still supposedly acting only in a constitutional manner.

'Kenyatta tells us to join K.A.U. and follow Jomo and the other leaders.

Chorus:
'Tell the elders to get out of our way, they caused our lands to be taken from us. Let the young men rise up instead and our lands will be returned.

'You Europeans are strangers here in the land of the black people, know in your hearts that the time is coming for you to go home.

'Those who sell themselves to the Europeans will be accursed by the house of Mumbi.

'Gikuyu was told, "I want you to dwell in this land which I show you, and all your descendants likewise".

'Even though you (Europeans) oppress us, the land is still ours, it was given us by God and we will never let it go.

'God will hear the prayers of Gikuyu. He will drive out the White Man and we black men will be left here.'

Hymn 30 is headed 'Soldiers of Jomo Kenyatta' and the chorus (shown as the third line of verse one, but used as a chorus to each of the other two-line verses) reads:

'Let us acclaim Kenyatta our "King", long may he live.'

The second line of verse four reads:

'You Europeans understand that you will leave by way of the sea.'

In verse six we have

'May God have mercy so that those who still slumber, may they awake so that we may all work for our war leaders that they may gain us the Kingdom.'

Hymn 32 starts off

'Let us all pray to God the Lord of War, and pray to him for power to conquer our enemy.'

Hymn 39 is a call to all the Kikuyu to rise up quickly as the lion (the leader) for whom they have been waiting for has appeared. Verse three reads:

'You Europeans, where did you get your good fortune, you have land in Europe but you want Kenya as well. When the day comes for our self-government, you will be destroyed. You traitors look out now lest you be burned with petrol.'

(We know all too well that this instigation to arson against the persons and property of loyalists has again and again been carried out.)

The last hymn in the book consists of two verses set to the tune of the British National Anthem, but consisting of a prayer by the Kikuyu for blessing on their land. This was the first venture in setting other words to the tune of 'God Save the King'. It enabled hundreds of Kikuyu to stand up to attention, with every appearance of great loyalty to the King, whenever the National Anthem was played, while, in fact, they were doing nothing more than pray for the return of their land.

As a test move it was most successful, for apparently no one in authority was aware of the new wording to the tune of 'God Save the King'. Instead there were many comments that the Kikuyu seemed to be more loyal to the Crown than ever before, judging by their behaviour when the National Anthem was played!

As already stated, there was yet another hymn-book which appeared only a few days after this one. Copies are not easy to obtain and I have not got one before me as I write, but I have notes from translations which I made in 1953. Perhaps the most significant thing about this particular book is that another set of words now appears, set to the tune of the National Anthem, which now becomes a heading 'Prayer for the King'. The words are a simple prayer, not for the King Emperor but for Jomo Kenyatta.

The following is a translation of the words:

'Pray unto God, praise God our father, pray for the one whom God has chosen to be our leader, that he shall lead us well. Say "Let him be wealthy", say "May our Kenyatta be victorious". With him are all those who agitate on behalf of the black people, all those who are working for self-government.'

Once the words of this version had been distributed to the Kikuyu members of K.A.U., members could show the greatest enthusiasm at the playing of the tune of our National Anthem, since for them it now became a straight prayer for the victory of Jomo Kenyatta over the enemy.

The 'Grey Book', as this issue of 20 August was often called, contains many hymns which are nothing but a call to the people to join K.A.U. (i.e. Mau Mau) in order that, by the strength of great numbers, there may be victory over the Europeans. Eight of them refer to K.A.U. by this name, others only by inference, or by direct reference to the known leading members of the movement.

Verses such as five of Hymn 6, which is headed 'Men of K.A.U. Listen', show that already the open aim of K.A.U. is to defeat and drive out the White Man. It reads:

'Pray to God to grant you his strength that you may overcome the Europeans in a great victory.'

Moreover, the threats to loyal Kikuyu who co-operate with the Europeans are no longer veiled, but very clearly show the relationship of K.A.U. with Mau Mau methods and plans. For example, verse eight of Hymn 9 runs:

'The day the Europeans go home all those who side with them will have their necks wrung like fowls.'

While verse nine of the same hymn reads:

'You leaders of K.A.U. we want you to know that we are all with you, so put away your fears.'

Hymn 20, in verse four refers to a mass meeting and says:

'The police of Nyeri were very afraid when they saw the K.A.U. flag hoisted.'

Hymn 29, which is a skit on the famous hymn, 'I trust in the Blood of Jesus', has as its chorus:

'I have planted myself firmly on the side of K.A.U.'

and then goes on in verse three to show *unmistakably* that K.A.U. is the same as Mau Mau, for this verse reads:

74

'I am made strong by the oath, the oath of the children of Mumbi.[1] I will never sell our land but remain on it for ever.'

If I have dwelt at considerable length on these skits on Christian hymns—set to Christian hymn-tunes—as the main Mau Mau method of spreading propaganda, it is because I feel that it is a subject of major importance. There is no doubt at all that these hymns, which were being sung at K.A.U. meetings, at Independent Schools and Churches, in the homes of thousands in the Kikuyu Reserve, in squatter villages on European farms, and even in the staff quarters and kitchens of European homes, were one of the most powerful propaganda weapons of the whole Mau Mau movement.

Europeans were inclined to look askance on their employees if they pored too diligently over any of the various vernacular newspapers, since they recognised them as the probable tools of subversive agitators. But what European, hearing well-known hymn-tunes such as 'Onward Christian Soldiers', 'Abide with Me', 'I am washed in the Blood of Jesus'—let alone the tune of the National Anthem—was likely to suspect that violent propaganda against himself was being spread by this means!

It was so simple and so effective. Administrators in all other tribes in Kenya, and indeed throughout Africa, would do well to pay particular attention to this clever Kikuyu method of subversive propaganda, under cover of what seems to be enthusiastic Christianity and loyalty to the Crown. It may well be copied and tried elsewhere.

Naturally the hymn-books were not the only propaganda instruments. The vernacular press was extensively used to the same end, but since the subversive leaders were well aware that the various Kikuyu newspapers were subject to

[1] The Mau Mau oath is regularly called 'the oath of the children of Mumbi', and here it is linked with K.A.U. in terms of complete unambiguity.

a close scrutiny by the Intelligence Branch of the Police, the propaganda published in these newspapers had to be much more carefully worded and veiled.

The Kikuyu, however, are past-masters in the use of parables, and of sentences which have a double meaning. Again and again anti-British propaganda and incitements to violence were so cleverly worded that it would be quite impossible to prove in a court of law that this was their intent. Yet their meaning was quite clear to every Kikuyu who read them.

The same thing was of course true of public speeches. The leaders knew full well that the police usually had observers posted to attend their meetings. They thus had to be careful in their wording, but could always so prepare parts of their speech in such a way that it would have a double meaning. If they were called on to explain this afterwards, they could always maintain that the innocent meaning was the one they had given to their words, even if every one knew that this was not the case.

It would be possible to discuss Mau Mau propaganda almost indefinitely, but enough has been said to indicate how diverse and how thorough it was. We must now pass on to consider some aspects of the oath ceremonies.

VI

MAU MAU OATH CEREMONIES

In the days before the State of Emergency was declared the ceremonies which accompanied the administration of the Mau Mau oath were simple and relatively harmless when compared to the many new, more elaborate and bestial accompaniments of the oath which have since been instituted.

Today there are at least seven, perhaps eight, grades of oaths and all the higher grades involve concomitant acts of incredible beastliness and depravity. Before passing to these advanced stages of the oath and of their effect upon those who are subjected to them, I must outline, a little more fully than I did in my earlier book, how the 'first oath' is administered and how it worked.

There are of course many legal and recognised forms of Kikuyu oath which are taken openly and in accordance with Native Law and Custom, in connection with litigation.

Quite apart from the fact that the Mau Mau oath, even in its simplest 'first oath' form, is illegal—through having been declared so by Government, it was also illegal from the point of view of Native Law and Custom. It borrowed elements and ideas from many recognised oath ceremonies, but it differed from all recognised oaths in so many ways that it could not be said to conform to Native Law and Custom in any way at all. The whole object of the first oath—an oath which the leaders intended should be administered to every single Kikuyu—man, woman, and child—was to obtain such a hold over each person through psychological fear, that they would at least be passive and not do anything in open opposition to Mau Mau, even if they did nothing to help it.

77

To this end the ceremony of the first oath was so arranged as to include all those magical and ritual elements which were known to have the most binding effect upon the minds of members of the tribe.

In very many Kikuyu religious ceremonies an arch of sugar-cane stems and banana leaves is used; more particularly so in the very solemn ceremonies of initiation from juvenile to adult status which accompany circumcision. To almost every adult Kikuyu the act of passing through an arch of this sort is intimately linked in the mind with the most solemn moments of his or her life; the time when he or she was finally admitted into adult status within the tribe—a step corresponding in its solemnity to Confirmation for a deeply religious Christian.

It is not surprising, therefore, to find that the planners of the Mau Mau oath, which was to lead those who took it into a great brotherhood of the elect, arranged as the first step in this procedure the passing of the candidate either voluntarily, or by force, through such an arch, with all its solemn ceremonial significance.

Nor is it surprising that among tens of thousands of Kikuyu the taking of the first oath is so often thought of and spoken of as 'being initiated'—as something comparable to the great step which they had taken earlier in their lives when they were admitted to adult status, adult responsibilities, and adult privileges.

To heighten the effect upon the minds of their adherents, Mau Mau leaders specifically taught their followers that this was 'the new initiation' and that, unless they took the first Mau Mau oath, they could never hope to share in all the benefits and privileges that were later to come to all 'true Kikuyu'.

Unless they went through 'the new initiation' ceremony, and unless they could prove that they had done so, they would no longer rank as true 'children of the House of Mumbi and Gikuyu'. Instead they would be as despised as people who had never taken part in the traditional initiation ceremonies of the tribe. The mere act of passing through the ritual arch had the effect of preparing those who did so, mentally, for something solemn and binding, in a way that probably few, if any, Europeans can ever fathom.

Furthermore, in the normal traditional initiation ceremonies from childhood to adult status, the candidates at a certain stage in the proceedings had a necklet made from a special type of grass put over their necks. This therefore was also made into the second step in the ceremony of the first oath of Mau Mau and also had the effect of creating in the minds of the persons so treated a sense of solemnity and of the great ceremonial significance of what was soon to follow.

We see, then, that the ceremony of the first Mau Mau oath starts with two items of procedure which are included to impress upon the subject the solemnity of the occasion.

In the case of persons to whom the oath was about to be administered without their prior consent (and this was true of the majority of those to whom it was administered), they were made to pass through the arch in darkness (feeling it but not seeing it), and it was only after they were through it that the lights were turned up and they could see what had already happened. Then, while still mentally stunned by this first event, the grass necklet was put round their necks.

To anybody who knows the Kikuyu intimately the mental state of a person who had been subjected to these first two steps in the ceremony needs no further comment. To those who do not know them so well, it must be understood that they had undergone a very major mental shock. They had just performed solemn acts which were linked in their minds with initiation into full adult status, acts in which they had already participated in the past under

79

wholly different and entirely voluntary circumstances, acts which they never expected to repeat in all their lives.

The next step in the proceedings then would take place so quickly that they had no time to recover from the mental state they were in. A piece of roasted sacrificial meat was put to their lips and they were told to eat it. This was done seven times and between each mouthful they were made to repeat the words of the Mau Mau oath. If, as often happened, they refused to do so a sponsor spoke the words for them.

Next, blood was put to their lips seven times as the oaths were repeated. Then a small half gourd full of blood was passed round their head seven times, after which they were required to pierce a sodom apple with seven thorns and also to insert a thorn seven times into the eye of the sacrificial animal, which had been removed and placed ready on a leaf.

While the first two items of this procedure were, as we have seen, linked with the solemn rites of initiation, the placing of seven sacrificial pieces of meat to the lips and the smearing of the lips seven times with blood were items of procedure linked with genuine and legal oath ceremonies and were well known as such and to have a binding effect.

The piercing of the sodom apple with seven thorns, and the piercing of the sheep's eye with thorns as well as the passing of a calabash of blood round the head were, however, linked with something quite different; they were procedures linked most definitely with black magic and with the casting of evil spells.

Seven, moreover, is the number linked in Kikuyu minds with bad luck, and with magic rites and with oath ceremonies of a very severe nature, so that the performance of various rites seven times added potency of its own to all the other aspects of what was done.

In the earlier days of Mau Mau, the ceremony was concluded with the cutting of seven small incisions upon the arm or wrist of the person to whom the oath had been administered. This was intended as an outward and visible sign of the initiation into the 'new Kikuyu brotherhood', in just the same way that the physical act of circumcision was, and is, the outward and visible sign of initiation into full adult status and responsibilities in Kikuyu law. But once the authorities had discovered the facts about this outward and visible sign of Mau Mau membership it was quickly discontinued as being too dangerous.

As I said in my earlier book on the Mau Mau, the taking of the first Mau Mau oath was, as much as anything, aimed at making the masses at least 'passive' in their attitude to the secret organisation. Most of the oath clauses at this stage were negative and not positive and therefore so much easier to fulfil, by the simple process of doing nothing.

'I will not give away the secrets of this Society.'
'I will not help Government apprehend members of this Society.'
'I will not sell our land to strangers.'

But there were also some positive clauses even in the first oath ceremony, such as:

'I will help the society, when called upon to do so, with funds.'
'I will, if called upon to do so, render any help to members of the society that I am asked to do.'

The second oath ceremony resembled the first in nearly all matters of detail, but to it were added a number of much more positive clauses. Here it should be noted that as the number of oath administrators grew, so did the variations in the wording of the oath. Some oath administrators regularly combined the clauses of the first and second oath into a single ceremony, so that we come across many records of persons who, when describing how they took the Mau Mau oath *for the first time*, mention many of the clauses which are, more properly, clauses of the second stage of membership.

This was not (so far as I know) strictly in accordance with the instructions of the leaders, which seem to have been that every possible step (including trickery, cajolery, and threat) should be used to make every Kikuyu take the first oath, but that the second and subsequent oaths should only be administered to selected persons—people who had shown by their behaviour after the first oath that they were interested in the movement and willing to go further in it.

In the second oath—properly speaking—the person to whom it was administered, willingly and with their full prior consent (at least in so far as attending the ceremony was concerned), had to promise:

1. 'If I am called upon to do so, with four others, I will kill a European.'
2. 'If I am called upon to do so, I will kill a Kikuyu who is against the Mau Mau, even if it be my mother or my father or brother or sister or wife or child.'
3. 'If called upon to do so, I will help to dispose of the body of a murdered person so that it may not be found.'
4. 'I will never disobey the orders of the leaders of this society.'

By no means all of those who voluntarily agreed to *attend* a second oath ceremony were aware of the nature of the promises they would be required to take, and many refused point-blank to speak these words (which in the second ceremony could not be spoken by a sponsor or by proxy). If they thus refused they were very quickly threatened, and subjected to physical violence. If they still refused, they were killed in the presence of the others attending the ceremony, thereby ensuring that the others fully realised that the threats were not empty words.

Mau Mau could ill afford Government getting to know the details of the first oath. Still less could they afford to have any person who had attended at a second oath ceremony get away without having taken it and report on what had occurred. Therefore those who refused had to die, and no one will ever know how many of the thousands of 'missing' Kikuyu have died in this way.

Nevertheless, such was the hatred of the Mau Mau plan to murder Europeans and loyal Kikuyus, in the minds of many who went on to the second oath (without knowing beforehand what they were going to be asked to do) that many, after taking it, did go and report to the authorities. Of these, I regret to say, very many were later murdered by Mau Mau, in retaliation.

Whereas both the first and second oaths were being administered before the State of Emergency was declared, I do not think that the third oath was, or any of the subsequent stages, which at that time had not even been invented.

It is perhaps necessary to note at this point that both the first and the second oaths could be taken more than once. If this was done it merely reinforced the oath stage taken, it did not count as a higher stage.

Again and again leading Mau Mau personalities, having beguiled friends to a place where the first oath was to be administered, would go in with their 'victim' and take the oath, to show him how simple and harmless it was, if only he would not resist.

To the European it seems almost unbelievable that the taking of an oath to kill a European or a loyal Kikuyu—perhaps a close relative—could have the effect of making otherwise reasonable people actually perform such terrible deeds of violence.

Perhaps it is well that we should remember the effects of magic and witchcraft upon peoples in Great Britain only a few centuries ago; remember too how the fear of magic and witchcraft is still rampant in parts of Europe among the peasantry and not even quite dead in Great Britain after twenty centuries of Christianity.

For a people who fifty years ago were still completely under the spell of witchcraft and magic; who can still die from the fear of a spell put upon them; or who can become ill and wilt away from the knowledge of having broken some rule which involves ceremonial uncleanliness, it is not surprising that the combination of elements used in Mau Mau oaths had a most terrible mental effect.

The fear of supernatural punishments that will follow the breaking of the oath are so much greater (for the majority at least) than the fear of physical consequences, such as imprisonment or a death sentence, that the first easily overcomes the second, until it almost ceases to exist in the awareness of the person concerned.

When to all this you add the religious aspects of Mau Mau that have been dealt with in an earlier chapter, and the effect of its perpetual propaganda, it is a little easier to comprehend what has happened.

It is not possible in this book to give full details of the horrible, filthy, and degrading acts which are involved in the more advanced Mau Mau oaths. To do so would be to ensure that this book was never published, or if it was, that it would probably be banned. It must suffice to say that every single thing done is of such a nature as to make the person doing it, an outcast, unclean—and in many cases uncleansable—and utterly degraded in the eyes of Native Law and Custom.

This is quite deliberate; it makes those who take these more advanced oaths unable to join in any normal social life with ordinary people and therefore binds them the more to those who have become as depraved and unclean as they are themselves.

It renders the people who have taken these oaths so abnormal and unnatural that, after what they have gone through, no act of arson or massacre, or disembowelling of victims, can seem to be anything but mild.

The principle seems to be that the more foul the acts you want your followers to perform, the more debased and unclean and abnormal must you first make them. You must transform them, mentally, from human beings to something far beastlier than any animal in creation.

Let it here be said, in fairness to the early leaders of the Mau Mau movement, that I do not believe that any of them ever contemplated or in any way planned any of these more advanced oaths. They are the creation of some of the more abnormal and mentally deranged among those followers, who took over power and leadership when the earlier leaders—whose aims were evil enough—were arrested and detained.

It must also be clearly stated that the vast majority of Kikuyu—(for only relatively few have ever been called upon to take the more advanced stages of the oaths)— simply DO NOT BELIEVE that the things which are in fact being done in these ceremonies, are done. The acts are so unthinkable, that both loyal Kikuyu and many Mau Mau adherents, who have not gone so far along the path, just shake their heads and say 'it cannot be so'.

Yet there is a vast mass of proof that it is true, statements from men and women who have been subjected to these higher oaths and have since fallen into the hands of the authorities, and there is no doubt at all that it is because of these unspeakable advanced oaths that the 'hard core' perpetrates the fiendish acts which it does.

This naturally brings me to the question of whether such persons can ever be rehabilitated; by cleansing ceremonies, by pyschotherapy, by religion, or any other means.

So far as those who have only taken the first oath are concerned there is no question at all. The answer is 'yes'. Full and free confession followed either by a traditional cleansing ceremony, or by a genuine return to Christianity, results in a complete freedom from the supernatural fear that was engendered by the oath.

The same is true of the second oath and possibly also the third, although far fewer of those who have gone so far as the third oath ever really confess and seek cleansing and freedom from its effects.

But as regards the more advanced and more bestial and foul oaths, with all that they entail, I am much more doubtful. I would NOT say it was quite impossible, but I frankly do not see much chance of success. We may well have to face the necessity of segregating such people for the rest of their lives, so that the evil they have done and the knowledge of it eventually dies with them.

Many of the acts of defilement which are committed during the process of taking the more advanced oaths, are so utterly unthinkable to an ordinary Kikuyu that they are not the subject of any *specific* reference in Kikuyu Law and Custom. For this reason it is not possible to say 'By Kikuyu law there is no possibility of being cleansed from this act'. But most of what is done goes *far beyond the limits* of the sort of act which was regarded as so heinous that no cleansing was recognised by native law.

For instance, in Native Law and Custom incest with one's own mother was an act for which there was no purification. It resulted in the person concerned being outlawed for all time. Similarly, an unnatural sexual offence, committed with a ewe, rendered the person concerned uncleansable.

Both these crimes were regarded by law just as within the orbit of what might be done by very degenerate persons. Therefore they were taken into account and it was laid down that there was no possible cleansing from them. The persons concerned became outlaws and outcasts for ever. It would seem to be a logical conclusion then that the performance of still more revolting acts, acts which were so inconceivable to the Kikuyu mind that they were never taken into account in drawing up Kikuyu law, must, *ipso facto*, be still more incapable of being absolved by any cleansing ceremony.

In some of the more advanced Mau Mau oaths, not one, but a whole series of different revolting acts are performed, and I cannot conceive that a person who has sunk so low would ever be accepted back into normal Kikuyu society.

The whole object of these advanced oath ceremonies is to make the person who takes part in them so debased and brutish, that thereafter he will not shirk from any act whatsoever, such as the disembowelling of pregnant women, the cutting up of babies, and even still worse atrocities.

If those who planned these concomitants of the advanced oaths had thought that there was any way of being cleansed from them, they would not have used them, for their whole object would have been defeated.

It must be stressed that the details, both of procedure and of the words used, at oath ceremonies are always very variable, and that no attempt has been made by Mau Mau to standardise them. Even the phraseology of the words of the oaths differ greatly as between one ceremony and another, *because they have not been given any set form on paper.*

Moreover, when accounts of what happened at an oath ceremony are reported to the police or to other authorities, it is usually done after the lapse of anything from several days to many weeks, and the person recounting what happened to them tells of the events and the words used as he remembers them, stressing those things which affected him most.

For this reason, while the general picture of what happens at oath ceremonies is always the same, in all the accounts that I have come across (and they are many) the details vary considerably. That is natural enough. If you were to ask ten or twenty people each to give you—from memory— an account of what was done and what was said at their

Confirmation, the overall picture would be the same in every case, but there would be many differences in respect of details, even though the conformity of what happens at Confirmation Service is much greater (because it follows a written and set form) than is the case of Mau Mau oath ceremonies.

Then again, when a person who has gone through a Mau Mau oath ceremony decides to go and report about it to the authorities, he is usually concerned with giving a report about those parts of it which revolted him. Few fail to mention that they were asked to swear to murder members of their own family, or to give unfailing obedience to the organisation. Most accounts, however, *never* mention those parts of the ceremony that deal with morals.

But Mau Mau, as a religion, has to have a moral code of some kind, otherwise it would not fulfil the criteria which the minds of the masses demand in a religion. Having decided to oppose the Christian doctrine and teaching while retaining the outward form to some extent, they have substituted a moral code of their own. In the main the code is based upon the customs of the tribe in the olden days with modifications to suit changing conditions.

For this reason I think it may be worth while to give a full translation of a report written down by a Kikuyu himself, on the day following his admission into the movement at a combined first and second oath ceremony.

Here it is. It contains much that may seem irrelevant, but its interest lies in the fact that it was not a statement about an oath ceremony recorded by a Police Officer, investigating with a view to a prosecution. It is simply a straightforward factual account by a person who felt the urge to record what he had been through, never dreaming one day it would appear anonymously in print.

'On Monday, in the evening, I was at the home of a youth called A, son of B, and at about 7.30 while we were sitting chatting in his home, his mother came and called him outside and spoke with him. When he came back he said to me, "Let's go and call on a young man at K——," and we set off to K—— and went to the home of a woman called B.N.

'We entered her hut, the one roofed with old petrol tins, but we were told not to sit down there and were escorted to a thatched hut and where we found the brother of A, son of B, whose name is C, son of A.

'We waited there a little time, perhaps twenty minutes, and then the son of the woman B.N., whose name is M, came in and he told us to remove from ourselves anything and everything we had on us that had a European origin. I had to remove my watch, my identity documents, my shoes and everything that I had in my pockets and I was told to hand them temporarily to M, son of B.

'Then, when we had divested ourselves of all these things, we were escorted to another thatched hut. The youth who was with me, A, son of B, was taken there first and I was left in the other hut. When I was fetched by the young man called M, son of B, he was accompanied by three other men. M, son of B, seized me from behind and he was carrying a sword in his hand; the other three, each armed with a pistol, surrounded me. They took me to the second grass thatched hut where I found A, son of B, standing, having also been taken there.

'We had to wait about another twenty minutes at this place while a group of women were taken off "to be initiated". Then, when the women were done, I and four other males were fetched and we were conducted to the place where the ceremonies were taking place, which proved to be the house roofed with old petrol cans. We were forced to enter and the door was then locked.

'First of all I and the youth, A, son of B, were pushed forward, but before we got right to the place of cere- monies, I was seized by the throat and strangled till I could hardly breathe. Then they let me breathe and said, "You, don't you imagine you can come here with your eyes watching what is happening so as to go off and report it and give the names of those of us here". Then they hit me and then hit me again, on my face. They punched me with their fists in my ribs, and finally roughly pushed me towards where the ceremonies were taking place.

'This is what I saw; an arch made of all the things of importance to the Kikuyu and I had to pass through it seven times; there were also seven "sodom apples" there. After I had passed through the arch seven times I was taken off to the side where there were some other young men, while the same thing was done to A, son of B. He was then made to come and stand on my left side.

'Then they put some objects round our necks and a small piece of rawhide on our wrists and we were made to hold sodom apples in our left hands.

'Then the master of ceremonies picked up a small half gourd, which had blood in it, and addressed us, telling us to repeat whatever he said. First we had to each say:

'"I am so and so, son of so and so," to identify ourselves by our names; then, having done so, we had to repeat:

'"I speak here, before God and before the Council, and I say that if I fail to agree to all that it orders me to do"—then he paused and made us drink blood from the half gourd, then we had to go on:

'"I say that I speak here before God and before the Council and that I speak the truth; if I ever turn against the black people, or if I ever betray them to their enemies, may this oath destroy me." Then we had to drink more blood. Then we went on:

'"I speak the truth before God and before this Council and I say truthfully that if I now fail to become Kikuyu of the house of Gikuyu and Mumbi, that we may unite to save our country of Kikuyu which God gave unto us, and if I fail to obey all future orders given to me, may this oath destroy me."

'Then we had to drink blood again. Next he put down the gourd with blood in it and picked up some bits of meat and we each had to take a bit from it and swallow it and we had then to say: "If I should ever take part in the Christian Revival Meetings, may this oath destroy me." Then we were made to take another bite of the meat and say: "If I should ever be ordered to bring the head of my mother or my father, or my sister or brother or of a person who is an enemy of our people and should I fail to do so, may this oath destroy me; may it destroy me if I fail to carry out that order fully.

'"If I should be chosen to go and join the forest gangs, to act on behalf of our people, and if I should fail to obey such an order, may this oath destroy me.

'"If I should be called upon at night, or during a storm, by one of our people, and told to go with him, if I fail to do so may this oath destroy me.

'"If I ever again drink English beer, may this oath destroy me.

'"If I should ever go with a prostitute, may this oath destroy me.

'"If I should ever have sexual contact with a Kikuyu girl in the open, instead of taking her to the Thingira[1] hut, in accordance with old Kikuyu custom, may this oath destroy me.

'"If I should ever cause a girl to become pregnant and then not marry her, may this oath destroy me.

'"If I marry and thereafter seek divorce, may this oath destroy me."

'Then when these things were completed I was told to hold my hand up and say:

' "All these things which I have said I now confirm that I mean them with all my heart before God and before this Council. If I fail to observe these promises may this oath destroy me."

'Then we were all made to stand up together (I and all those who had taken the oath), and we all had to hold hands joining a circle. We had to have our eyes open and look up to the ceiling; when we were ready the elders M and N led us in prayer as follows:

[1] By Kikuyu law a young man could take a girl to the Thingira hut and spend the night with her, provided that he did actually have sexual intercourse with her. In the Thingira hut there were always other persons, to whom the girl would appeal if the youth attempted to do anything that was forbidden.

'"Lord God we pray you that you will cause the things we have spoken here tonight to be true and to take a firm hold in our hearts. Let none of us here depart from these paths, but rather may we all sincerely become servants serving our country which God gave unto us, that we may, as one man, when the time comes, to drive out the Europeans, and all help each other to do so. Praise, praise to God, praise."

'Then the elder M spoke and addressed us all, saying: "There is one thing I wish to impress upon you all. You have performed these rites tonight, if by any chance you took part in them in order to have information about them to take to your masters, do not imagine you can do so. We would know all about the reports you were making by the time you had signed your statements, for, I tell you, when you hear that so and so has been killed by a murderer and that the murderer was wearing police uniform, often it happens that he is not only wearing police clothes but actually was a policeman; for we have many, who are employed by Government, but who are actually on our side.

'"Nothing that happens fails to reach our ears, whenever anything happens there is always someone near, who is on our side, who brings us the news. Even from Europe there is no news that concerns us that does not reach us, whether it be about something that has happened, or about something that is being planned against us. You should all know and understand this. Moreover, if a man does report on us and then tries to deny it, we simply say 'We do not recognise him, let his life be extinguished, he is not one of us'."

'"Now come let us go and eat meat, while we write down the subscriptions, for the hour is far advanced and we ought to scatter to our homes."

'We then went across to the private quarters of B.N., going to her place from the place where the ceremonies had been performed, and we were served with meat and drink, after which they wrote down what each person paid and what he still owed. Then we went to our respective homes at about 12.30 midnight. Before we left we were told to come to another meeting, of which we would be informed, so as to receive further instructions and, as a parting word, we were reminded that if we failed to pay all monies demanded of us at any time, the oath would destroy us and if we were called upon to help dispose of a body and failed to do so, the oath would destroy us.

'Before we parted a man named N from over Githunguri way spoke briefly as follows:

' "When Kinuthia wa Mugia[1] was arrested I was appointed in his place, in accordance with Kenyatta's instructions. I spend my time in hiding, because if they caught me I would be sent to Kajiado![2] He gave me instructions how to help to acquire ammunition and weapons, if I got a chance." '

[1] The writer of one of the hymn-books, see page 55.
[2] The detention camp for Mau Mau leaders.

VII

MAU MAU METHODS

Mau Mau could clearly not have done all that it has done in the way of resistance to the armed forces and impudent acts of murder in the heart of the towns and cities if its followers had not had fire-arms, in addition to swords and spears. It is certain that stockpiling of arms and ammunition for Mau Mau purposes must have started a good many years before the State of Emergency was declared and that is one of the reasons, among others, why, from the outset, Mau Mau tried to enlist into its membership as many domestic servants as possible. Most Europeans had a fire-arm of one sort or another, many had several—sporting rifles, shotguns, revolvers and pistols—while few kept a close check upon their ammunition or locked it up.

Once the idea of stockpiling in these things was born, it was relatively easy for domestic servants, who had joined Mau Mau, to steal one or two rounds at a time—only the theft of bigger quantities was likely to be noticed—and gradually help to build up the hidden stocks that were needed by the movement. Theft of weapons presented a more difficult problem, for such thefts would be noticed much more quickly, and if too many disappeared before Mau Mau plans were ready, it would have made the authorities very suspicious. Nevertheless, a good many were, in fact, stolen in the years prior to the Emergency, and by no means all these thefts seem to have been reported to the police.

As soon as Mau Mau was out in the open, the organised theft of arms was at once greatly accelerated and reached very serious proportions; so serious, in fact, that the Government had to impose new and very strict penalties for the loss of fire-arms and ammunition. But even these measures did not succeed in making owners sufficiently careful to cut down the supply. This year, therefore, in its attempt to close the door more firmly, Government has reviewed all fire-arm licences and very many weapons have been compulsorily called in and taken charge of by the authorities.

When Mau Mau found that it could not obtain all the fire-arms that it required by theft, an organisation was started, within the movement, for the manufacture of home-made guns. Very great ingenuity has been shown in this process, but most of the guns so made are not very lethal, unless at very close quarters, nor will the barrels stand up to the firing of more than a very limited number of rounds.

Many of the attacks on Kikuyu home-guard posts, and on police stations (like the famous raid on Naivasha), have had, as their main objective, simply and solely the purpose of obtaining arms and ammunition to replenish dwindling stocks.

Mau Mau set up a special organisation within the movement composed of ex-convicts and known criminals, who were promised help and also handsome rewards in return for their services. One of the principal objectives of this group was the theft of weapons and ammunition. Members of the movement whose duties gave them a chance to know where Europeans kept their weapons, and what they did with them at different times of the day and night, were required to pass on the information, at once. The organisation responsible for arms-collecting would then delegate the job of stealing to a suitable operator, supplying him with all the necessary information. When, as so often happened, a European or Asian carelessly left a gun, or a supply of ammunition, in a car, any Mau Mau adherent who saw it had to pass on the information at once. Ordinary members who saw objects lying unattended in a car were not expected to steal them themselves. To do so would be foolish, as they would have no knowledge of how to dispose of them to the right quarter, quickly, without trace. Their job was simply to pass on the information quickly, so that an 'operator' could immediately be detailed to carry out the actual theft, and pass the proceeds to the right quarter.

As an adjunct to the illegal acquisition and use of fire-arms, there came a well-planned system for hiding and concealing them, and it must be admitted that, on many occasions, security force search parties have missed arms and ammunition when they have been within a few yards, or even feet, of hidden supplies. The making of a really thorough search of any premises is a very skilled operation and one which only very highly trained personnel can carry out properly. Unfortunately, it became necessary to recruit a very large number of men for the police at short notice and to use them with somewhat inadequate training, so that the Mau Mau had a big advantage when it came to concealing ammunition and weapons.

The sort of places that have been successfully used include charcoal-burning irons and charcoal braziers, all ready to be lit, and put so openly near the door of the room that the searchers have looked everywhere in less obvious hiding-places, and found nothing.

Another type of hiding-place that was used most successfully, for a time, in Nairobi was in the Municipal dust-bins, in the Native Locations. The people knew well the exact hours when the bins were emptied by the dust and rubbish carts, and, as soon as a bin had been emptied and the carts had moved on, weapons and ammunition would be put into the bins and lightly covered with some refuse, specially kept for the purpose. As the day went on, more rubbish would be put in, in the normal way, and shortly before the next time for clearance, the weapons would be temporarily moved, to be returned again to this most safe hiding-place.

Once the authorities discovered this particular trick, word was passed round very quickly that dust-bins were no longer safe for this purpose, and fresh instructions were issued.

As a part of the illegal arms business, it became necessary to have all sorts of special code words, so that verbal and written messages could be sent about the stealing, hiding, or distribution of fire-arms, that would be clear to the recipient, but not appear in the least suspicious to the ordinary security investigator.

While the need for arms and ammunition supplies has for long been one of Mau Mau's major preoccupations, the need for funds has been fully as important. To start with, the organisation had very little difficulty in getting all the money that it needed by voluntary subscription. The specious promises about the recovery of lost land, and the distribution of land now owned by European farmers to members of the movement, when the battle was won, were excellent inducements to a free flow of money to the party funds—*so long as they were believed.*

Money was very badly needed; it was needed to pay the top-ranking organisers of the movement, and supply their travelling expenses. It was needed to finance the printing of newspapers, leaflets, and the propaganda 'hymn-books'. It was needed to pay allowances to the families of any Mau Mau member who had the misfortune to be arrested and imprisoned or detained. It was needed, in great quantity, for the families of the men who had gone into the forests to become members of the fighting forces of the movement. It was needed for a whole host of other purposes such as buying equipment, medical supplies, food, and for rewards to the criminals who stole weapons and ammunition. Much money was also needed for the legal defence of Mau Mau leaders who were being prosecuted.

Before very long, the money raised by subscription ceased to be sufficient for the needs of the movement, and, particularly so, after Mau Mau and the Kenya African Union were proscribed and it became illegal to pay subscriptions to these bodies.

At about the time when funds were beginning to drop off badly, and when some members were openly refusing to pay their dues, Mau Mau decided to institute its own system of 'courts' for the punishment of members. To start with, these 'courts' were chiefly concerned with imposing minor fines upon members for breaches of rules and it was soon found that this was an excellent way of replenishing the dwindling funds.

The 'courts' then decided that even more money could be made by bringing before the 'courts', wealthy members of the tribe—especially traders—who were not members of Mau Mau, and making it clear to them that if they did not agree to pay substantial fines (sometimes running into amounts of £250 or more), the 'courts' would sentence them to death.

At first, this threat tended to be ignored, but when it became known that they were not idle threats at all, and that a number of people had 'disappeared' after appearing before a Mau Mau 'court', and had later been discovered either strangled or mutilated, the position changed. Thereafter the 'courts' became a really sure source of funds for the party, since few who came before them preferred the risk of violent death to the payment of a fine, however unjust or exorbitant.

A new problem now faced Mau Mau and that was how to keep their funds safe and so covered that the authorities would not suspect the origin or the intended use of the money, and confiscate it.

In the earlier days, subscription lists were kept, receipts for funds collected and subscriptions paid were issued, and most of the money was banked in the name of the Kenya African Union, or personally by certain leaders, and by treasurers of party funds. But, after the State of Emergency was declared, the matter became more difficult. It was dangerous to have too much money in loose cash, but it could no longer be banked with the older accounts. New ways and means of banking it, without raising suspicion, had therefore to be organised.

Bogus trading companies and social organisations, such as Musical Societies, were formed and Mau Mau funds were kept as though it was either company monies, or subscriptions and donations to societies which on their face had nothing whatever to do with Mau Mau.

Even when the authorities guessed that such subterfuges as these were being employed, it was often very hard to prove that such money was nothing more than funds illegally collected, for an equally illegal purpose.

The public, both in Kenya and Overseas, is often much puzzled why relatively few cases are recorded of Mau Mau illegal 'courts of justice', and Mau Mau 'oath ceremonies' being surprised in session by the security forces, so that the people concerned in such acts can be dealt with according to the law. The answer, of course, lies in the very highly organised Mau Mau warning system. Whenever a Mau Mau 'court' is about to go into session, or a Mau Mau oath ceremony is taking place, or a meeting of a local committee is being held, a complicated system of sentries is organised, covering all possible approaches to the scene. If any security forces in uniform appear anywhere near, or even if any strangers in plain clothes are seen, warning signals are at once passed on and the assembled persons scatter and all traces of what was going on are quickly hidden.

Even when information of a reliable character has been received that an oath ceremony or a secret meeting, or a 'court' session is due to be held at a particular place, at a given time, it is very hard indeed for the forces of law and order to catch the culprits red-handed.

Now that the masses are increasingly turning against

Mau Mau and that quite a number of former adherents are beginning to change their allegiance, it sometimes happens that persons who have been appointed to such 'sentry duty' help the police. Successful raids are therefore becoming a little more frequent.

From the very beginning of the movement, many Mau Mau leaders maintained that one of the ways in which the Europeans could be defeated—since clearly defeat in open battle with the limited resources of arms and ammunition available to them was out of the question—was by making the position of the Europeans so uncomfortable and his economic position so precarious that the majority of white people would voluntarily pack up and go. To achieve this end, those who are responsible for the more active side of Mau Mau—the leaders of the forest gangs— have concentrated, to a considerable extent, upon harrying tactics and destruction. Incessant raids upon European-owned farms, the wicked hamstringing and maiming of valuable livestock, the burning of grain stores, raids on farm-houses involving in some cases the wanton massacre of the European occupants—all of these things are part of a plan to make life so uncomfortable for the European settler, that he will decide to leave Kenya and start life afresh, elsewhere.

To some extent the policy has succeeded and there have been a number of cases of Europeans deciding that 'Kenya is no place to stay and farm these days', or 'there is no future for the white man in Kenya now'. Those who have taken this line have undoubtedly played right into the hands of Mau Mau.

Fortunately, however, the vast majority of Europeans in Kenya are made of sterner stuff and are not prepared to lose heart. Certainly, the constant mental worry of never knowing whether you and your family will be the target for a sudden raid, never knowing whether when you come back from some job that has taken you temporarily away from home, you may not find your family dead, your house in flames, and your cattle all mutilated, does have a very serious effect upon people.

So long as the security forces were more on the defensive, than actively on the offensive, the position from this point of view was very grave, but now it is the gangs that are being harried in all directions, and who never know when and from which direction they may be attacked next. In consequence the position is rapidly improving.

Mau Mau leaders have always had a great faith in the weapon of intimidation, and in this they have shown very bad judgment, on a number of occasions. The most outstanding mistake they ever made was the Lari massacre. In the Lari area there were a considerable number of anti-Mau Mau Kikuyu, who had steadfastly refused to take the Mau Mau oath or to help the movement in any way whatever. Firmly believing in their intimidation tactics, the leaders thought that they would do something really drastic and, by doing so, on the one hand kill off a body of people who had constantly opposed them, and on the other intimidate loyal anti-Mau Mau Kikuyu everywhere else, so that, in future, people would be more willing to come over to their side, even if only to save their skins.

No words of mine can describe the utter wanton brutality, the calculated cruelty, and the savagery of the Lari episode. Great numbers were slashed to death, or burned alive in their huts, many, many more were fearfully maimed for life. Pregnant women were disembowelled alive, and children sliced to death. But the effect of Lari was far other than the leaders had planned. As an act of intimidating the loyalists, it was a complete and utter failure.

As the news of the Lari massacre spread, Kikuyu, all over the country, including many who had previously supported the movement, were so revolted by what had happened that I believe it is true to say that Lari marked the turning-point in Mau Mau fortunes.

It is a strange, but true, fact, that whereas an individual can often be intimidated by threats of violence to himself, and more particularly to his family, the carrying out of major acts of violence against women ánd children has the reverse effect, and stiffens resistance to those perpetrators of such plans.

VIII

MAU MAU AND OTHER TRIBES

As I said in my earlier book, *Mau Mau and the Kikuyu*, Mau Mau was virtually the same as the earlier Kikuyu Central Association, which was finally banned in 1941. I also said that to the majority of Africans, and more particularly to the Kikuyu tribe, the terms K.C.A., Mau Mau, and K.A.U. (Kenya African Union) were synonymous. This has been more than substantiated by the evidence I have given in the earlier chapters of the present book.

This proven identity between the old K.C.A., Mau Mau, and K.A.U. (in its later stages) is of the very greatest importance when we try to assess the likelihood, or otherwise, of Mau Mau having a *serious* effect upon other tribes.

In the days before the Second World War, when the K.C.A. was becoming increasingly active—as well as increasingly subversive—very strenuous efforts were made to spread K.C.A. doctrines among other tribes. In order to do this, similar associations were set up (or where they existed, encouraged) among other tribes, and they were all granted affiliation to the K.C.A. as being the parent body as well as the most influential and active one.

In particular, strong associations were organised among the Kamba and Teita tribes, while close contact with, but less influence over, existing associations among the Luo, Bantu Kavirondo, Masai, and Kipsigis was maintained.

Undoubtedly, it was with the Kamba and the Teita that the old K.C.A. had its greatest successes, and it thus came about that when the K.C.A. was finally banned and its leaders detained during the war, the affiliated Kamba and

Teita organisations and their respective leaders shared detention with the K.C.A. organisers.

But whereas, in those days, the K.C.A. already had a fairly big following, with something like twenty-five branches, more than half of these were not in the Kikuyu Reserve at all, but in the White Highlands among the squatters. There were also branches in Northern Tanganyika among the Kikuyu who had emigrated there, and in Kikuyu settlements in Masai country and in the land of the Kisii.

The Kamba and Teita affiliated organisations never really obtained any great hold over the members of those tribes, in spite of all the efforts that were made to indoctrinate them. For a short time the Kamba organisation achieved a temporary great increase in membership when the controversy over de-stocking and soil conservation was raging, but the interest of the masses was not maintained.

After the release of the former K.C.A. leaders, as well as of the leaders of the affiliated organisations in Kamba and Teita at the end of the war, the K.C.A. men very quickly started reorganising in secret, and, in due course, the Mau Mau variant of K.C.A. was born. But among the Kamba and Teita, however, there was no similar recrudescence.

When the Kenya African Union—which had been originally founded in an attempt to bring together the politically-minded members of all the tribes in Kenya, to voice their views openly and constitutionally—gradually came more and more under the control of the former K.C.A. leaders, and as the Kikuyu came to dominate K.A.U., there was a marked change of policy by the Union.

Men in various tribes who had once been fellow-travellers with the K.C.A., and in close contact with its headquarters, were chosen, in many areas, as K.A.U. office-bearers, and a very definite attempt was then made to spread Mau Mau doctrines among tribes other than the Kikuyu. Meetings, held under the auspices of K.A.U. took place all over Kenya and the principal speakers were men who, at one and the same time, were the open and known leaders of K.A.U. and the secret organisers of the K.C.A. or Mau Mau movement.

Partial, but only partial, success was achieved. A certain number of the Akamba, in very limited districts of the tribal area, were attracted to the idea of an underground side to K.A.U., while a few ardent followers also appeared in Teita, at the Coast, and in Nyanza Province. But during all the years when Mau Mau was rapidly gaining ground among the Kikuyu, not only in the Land Unit but also wherever Kikuyu communities were to be found, only a very limited number of Africans of other tribes became adherents to the cause, in spite of all the efforts of Jomo Kenyatta and his disciples.

The only real successes were in Nairobi, and to a much less extent in other towns, where it was rather easier to win over members of the other tribes when they were living under conditions which led to a mental state of discontent and unrest.

Why was it that Mau Mau was able to get such a grip of the Kikuyu, while it had so much less effect upon the other tribes? Various factors have, in my opinion, played their part.

In the first place, the Kikuyu, for a variety of reasons set out in my earlier book, had more genuine grievances which could be magnified and exaggerated and used to work up feeling of anger against Europeans. Secondly—and I think this is a point of considerable importance—the real leaders of the movement were Kikuyu individuals with very considerable personality and qualities of leadership. The impact of these qualities naturally had a much greater effect upon their own people than upon members of other tribes. While other tribes do not necessarily lack men with similar powers of leadership and personality, the fact remains that those self-styled leaders of other tribes who did throw in their lot with the Kikuyu Mau Mau leaders were men of a very different calibre, and who in consequence were *not* able to have the same effect upon their people, as Mau Mau leaders had on the Kikuyu.

The Kamba were more affected than other tribes simply because they were more closely related to the Kikuyu and have a very similar language and customs. The Kikuyu leaders could, and did, use therefore their personality to influence them. But this the Kikuyu leaders could not do to the Luo or to the Bantu Kavirondo, for at heart—despite all the talk of African unity—the Luo and other tribes in Nyanza hate and despise the Kikuyu, and will never be led by them.

Had the Mau Mau Kikuyu leaders been able to find a Luo with magnetic personality who would join cause with them, I think the outcome might have been very different. The Luo might then have joined in, in a big way, at least at the start. I doubt, however, if the Luo have the tenacity of purpose (which has always been a strong Kikuyu characteristic) which would have enabled them to carry on against organised security forces for very long, if they decided to throw in their lot with Mau Mau.

With the Kamba the position is different. In parts of Kamba country there is, to my mind, a very definite potential danger, for, like the Kikuyu, they are a tenacious people. But the Kamba have, for years, supplied very large numbers of men to the Police Force and the Army so that Kamba country is full of retired members of these two forces. These men know, from personal observation, what the power of the White Man is and what his organisation in time of war can be like, and they are not easily going to allow their fellow-tribesmen to get involved in anything comparable to Mau Mau. They know it could not succeed, while the Kikuyu, in their ignorance, genuinely believed that they could.

Where Mau Mau influence has made itself most felt upon other tribes is in Nairobi where members of all the different tribes mix with each other much more freely, without the hindrances which tribal custom exerts, in the Native Land Units.

In Nairobi there is no doubt whatever that individual members of very many tribes have joined the Mau Mau organisation—mostly through K.A.U. when that body was functioning. For this reason, the Mau Mau organisation has used Nairobi as a sort of training-ground for men and women of other tribes who will spread the doctrine into other areas.

As the drive against the Kikuyu members of the Mau Mau organisation, within Nairobi, was intensified, it was most useful to have members who were not subject to all the special regulations that were imposed upon individuals of the Kikuyu, Embu, and Meru tribes. They could serve as couriers and as guardians of secret documents. They could be asked to take charge of, and hide, arms and ammunition, since the risk of search of their houses by the police was very much less.

Once members of other tribes had been persuaded to join Mau Mau in Nairobi, they were asked to work out their own tribal variants of the Mau Mau oath ceremonies, and there is no doubt that both Luo and Kamba variants have been devised and put into use to a limited extent.

Fortunately, when such agents do go back to their own tribal areas, there are usually plenty of people who are not slow to report that subversive activities are starting, and so the chances of spreading the movement secretly, in other tribes, are not very great.

In Tanganyika Territory, the former branches of the Kikuyu Central Association, especially in the Northern Province, have certainly established links with small, discontented groups of people in the other tribes, and although membership of Mau Mau was probably confined to Kikuyu, Embu, and Kenya Meru who had settled in Tanganyika, they seem to have a good many sympathisers among local people who believe that Kikuyu leadership might help them in getting some of their own grievances against the European put right.

In the days before the war and before the Kikuyu Central Association was banned, links had been established by that body with the leaders of a number of African political associations in Uganda, and there is no doubt that these links were renewed and maintained, after the war, ostensibly through the K.A.U. organisation. Contacts between Kikuyu and Baganda have been made easier and more natural than similar contact between other tribes, because each is the most advanced tribe within the respective country and each has probably more members who have been to England. Many of the political leaders of these two tribes have been overseas and many contacts were made while out of their own country.

If it were not for the fact that I think the Baganda masses are psychologically not the right type to go in for the Mau Mau type of activity on a big scale (or to carry it on for more than a short time, if they did start), I should be more likely to expect an outbreak of Mau Mau among them than almost anywhere else in East Africa.

It is in Northern Tanganyika, on the other hand, that there are tribes with a similar mental outlook and tenacity of purpose as the Kikuyu, and if they were to become seriously affected by Mau Mau doctrines they might take to the movement, very much as the Kikuyu did three years ago, using very similar methods.

If the Mau Mau movement had not been forced into the open at the time when the State of Emergency was declared, before its plans were ready, and if it had had, therefore, a greater measure of initial success, the spread to other tribes and other areas might have been a very real threat. But because Mau Mau went off at half-cock, and because other tribes have seen the misery, poverty, and terror that Mau Mau has brought to the Kikuyu tribe, I think that the present generation in other tribes (with the exception of small groups of extremists) will be very reluctant to enlist in anything similar.

I am afraid, however, that Mau Mau's methods of propaganda, which have been studied, and carefully learnt by a small handful of embittered men of various other tribes, will be tried out elsewhere in ten or fifteen years' time, when a generation has grown up that has no personal memory of the disaster which it brought upon the Kikuyu. That is why, in the final chapters of this book, I shall indicate measures which I believe must be taken as a matter of urgency in order that this may never happen.

IX

KIKUYU 'LOYALISTS' AND HOME GUARDS

Although the Security Forces—represented by the Police and the Military in all their diverse branches—are naturally playing a very big part against the militant Mau Mau, the people who are in most constant opposition to them, through being in the closest contact, are the Kikuyu Home Guards. This body is, in the main, composed of 'loyalists', as those Kikuyu who are opposed to Mau Mau are locally termed.

This designation 'loyalist' is often misunderstood outside Kenya and is wrongly thought to indicate people who whole-heartedly support the policy of Government and of the Europeans in general. This is not quite the true position. I would say, rather, that the 'loyalists' are people who disapprove most strongly of Mau Mau's methods of trying to achieve their objective and who disagree, too, in part with Mau Mau aims and objects.

It would be wholly wrong, however, to think of the 'loyalists' as out-and-out supporters of the policy of Europeans in Kenya. On the other hand they are completely loyal to the Crown, as represented by Her Majesty the Queen.

By far the greatest number of 'loyalists' are either Christians or out-and-out believers in the old religion of the Kikuyu. Among the latter are men like Chief Njiri, who has no sympathy with Christianity, but who considers that Mau Mau transgresses against all his most cherished beliefs and can only bring down the anger of 'Mwene Nyaga' and of the ancestral spirits upon the Kikuyu tribe.

The leaders of the 'loyalists' include men from all walks of life, political leaders like Harry Thuku—the President of the Kikuyu Provincial Association—and his district

Vice-Presidents, the leader of the 'Torch Bearers', Mr. Parminas Keritu, who is a great personal friend of Harry Thuku, a number of important Government chiefs, a few prominent Kikuyu traders and men of commerce, and most of the ordained Kikuyu clergy and pastors of the various Missions, Catholic, Protestant, and Nonconformist alike.

In earlier days there was a good deal of friction between many of these men. The chiefs resented the political fame of men like Harry Thuku, the clergy disapproved of chiefs who were not adherents of the Christian faith, the traders were rather aloof from everybody and concerned only with their own business affairs. But opposition to the methods of Mau Mau has welded these people together into a strong body that is leading public opinion in the tribe to turn away from the evil that is destroying their country. All of them are, above all else, Kikuyu patriots, whose one real aim is to help build up a strong and united Kikuyu people, who will go forward together to real progress and prosperity.

These leaders include some of the most intelligent (though not necessarily the most educated, in the academic sense) personalities of the tribe, men who realise that progress will only be achieved by co-operation with the White Man. They sincerely believe that the many reforms which they would like to see brought about can be achieved by negotiation with Government on a constitutional basis, not by violent opposition to it.

I have been privileged to attend numerous meetings when these 'loyalists'' leaders, drawn from all walks of life, have met to discuss ways and means of combating Mau Mau and restoring peace to their people. At every such meeting the opportunity has been taken to discuss long-term problems, not affecting the immediate one of defeating Mau Mau, and to put forward recommendations about them for Government's consideration.

To me, this new co-operation between good chiefs and the level-headed political leaders, between prominent clergy and professional traders, is one of the most encouraging signs and much of the future progress of the tribe will depend upon the continuance of this relationship between these different sections of the community. If they were united only by their common hatred of Mau Mau, they might easily cease to co-operate once Mau Mau was at an end. But their deliberations have shown, again and again, that they have realised the contribution each group has to make to the common cause of Kikuyu progress and I think that they will continue to work together in the future, when Mau Mau has been overcome.

It is against the 'loyalists', of all types, that Mau Mau's flagging army is fighting its hardest. It is the 'loyalists' whom the Mau Mau really hate and who are therefore the target for the worst brutalities. The official record of the number of 'loyalists' who have been foully murdered is well over 1,200, but this figure falls far below actuality. It represents only those known to have been killed. 'Loyalists' themselves reckon that for every one person officially listed, there must be at least three who have simply disappeared, quietly strangled on a dark night, and the body disposed of by burying.

Mau Mau leaders know full well that the real cause of the failure of their plans has little to do with Government; it was the 'loyalists' who were responsible. Men like the late Chief Waruhiu (who was murdered just before the State of Emergency was declared), Harry Thuku, the Rev. Wanyoike, and many others set to work, long before the State of Emergency, to force Mau Mau into the open and make it show its hand. Their object was to see to it that it never reached—in secret—the appointed day when a sort of *coup-d'état* was to be achieved, and those who did not follow the movement, together with all Europeans, would be eliminated in one night of horror.

The unfailing courage of the 'loyalists'' leaders has been a magnificent example to the rank and file of those who are opposed to Mau Mau and, gradually, with the help of the leaders, a strong force of what is called 'Home Guards' has been built up.

To start with, these groups were unco-ordinated and unarmed and were mainly working as patrols to give the alert if a gang showed up and, also, as a sort of intelligence service to help collect facts about Mau Mau activities in their district.

Gradually, however, more organisation was possible. British leaders for the Home Guard were appointed, arms and ammunition were supplied, a modicum of training was given, and the force began to make itself felt.

Inevitably, once the Home Guards were given arms and ammunition, they became an immediate target for the gangsters, since there was always a bigger chance of being able to destroy a small Home Guard post and capture its weapons and ammunition than there was of success against the better organised police and military posts.

Moreover, as soon as the policy of arming the Home Guards got under way, every attempt was made by the leaders of the Mau Mau movement to get some of their own followers enlisted in the group. This was for two purposes: on the one hand they would be able to collect and pass on useful information about plans that were being made against the gangsters, while on the other hand they could act on the inside and help to seize weapons and arms when an attack was made by a Mau Mau gang upon a Home Guard defence post.

To some slight extent they succeeded and one of the problems that constantly faces the 'loyalist' leaders and the European officers of the Home Guard, is how to be sure of the absolute integrity of those who volunteer to join.

As the movement against the Mau Mau has grown in strength, people who were formerly Mau Mau adherents have openly rejected the movement and have gone over to join up with the Home Guards in the fight against their former colleagues, but with them have come, occasionally, persons who are posing as friends with a view to fifth-column activities.

As was to be expected, Mau Mau propaganda is constantly being launched at the people who belong to the Home Guard, in the hope of persuading them to change their allegiance. The families of Home Guards are continually under threat, and most of them therefore sleep, at night, in the Home Guard posts, which have defences against sudden attack.

Inevitably, in a force which is only partially trained and disciplined, there has been a certain amount of abuse of power. There have been reports of Home Guards using their position to pay off old scores that have nothing whatever to do with Mau Mau; reports of looting and theft during searches of homesteads for Mau Mau offenders. On the whole, however, I am less surprised at incidents of this sort that have happened, than at their relative rarity, under conditions where the temptation must often be very great.

The Home Guards are doing a very good job indeed, and they could do an even better if there were available more suitable Europeans as Home Guard leaders.

One of the tragedies of Kenya is the terrible lack of Kenya-born young men who can really speak any of the vernacular languages properly. Had these been available, even thirty or forty such men, when the Home Guard was being formed, the task of welding the volunteers for this service into a real power would have been very much easier.

If there is a lesson to be learnt from this, for the future, both in Kenya and in neighbouring territories, it is the need for encouraging young Englishmen, whether in the Police Force, or in the Administration, whether in business or on the farms, to learn one of the languges of the country really thoroughly, so that, if ever a similar emergency should arise, there would be more people available to help to lead the 'loyalists' in their fight against evil.

In addition to the out-and-out 'loyalist' leaders and the Home Guards, there is a considerable body of Kikuyu who are often described as 'sitting on the fence'. They are certainly not whole-hearted supporters of Mau Mau, although a very high proportion of them have probably taken the first simple Mau Mau oath. They have done this chiefly as a sort of 'insurance'.

In the early days of the movement so little appeared to be done by Government against Mau Mau, that a great many people, who had no active interest in it, felt that it was wise to join. Their only real interest was to go on with their normal day to day lives, to live and let live, and to enjoy themselves. But the Mau Mau movement could not be ignored and it was widely known that people who showed too much hostility were just 'disappearing'—quietly murdered and disposed of. These 'sitters on the fence' are now coming over increasingly to the side of the 'loyalists' because they can see that the Mau Mau cause is losing ground. They are, however, still very cautious and are careful not to appear too openly on the side of law and order, since their one object is to be unmolested so that they can carry on their normal lives.

Among those who are 'sitting on the fence' in this way, there are undoubtedly a good many headmen and a few chiefs. To the Mau Mau they can always say, 'Well, I have to appear to be on Government side since I am a Government servant, otherwise I would lose my job, but you know that really I try to help you as much as I can'.

To Government, if their activities against Mau Mau are not all that they might be, they can also present a reasonable excuse. 'We have tried', they will say, 'but circumstances are against us and somebody gave a warning to the people you sent us to arrest.'

These 'sitters on the fence' are undoubtedly a severe handicap to those fighting against Mau Mau, for they undoubtedly do not do nearly as much as they could to help destroy Mau Mau. They are so numerous that they cannot all be arrested and punished, and anyhow, it is almost impossible to prove that they have helped Mau Mau in any way, other than by being passive.

If more active steps could be taken to win these people over to whole-hearted support of Government, the end of Mau Mau resistance in the Reserve could be achieved much more quickly. But wherever there appears to be a major move by the 'sitters on the fence' towards supporting Government, Mau Mau leaders take immediate measures to crush such ideas, and those concerned then tend to revert to a state of helping neither one side nor the other.

X

THE HANDICAPS OF THE
SECURITY FORCES

People who do not understand what conditions are really like in Kenya, frequently ask how it is that Mau Mau has been able to hold out for so long against the combined forces of the Police, the Army, and Air Force, with their far greater resources of materials and superiority of weapons.

There are many different factors which contribute to the difficulties of operating successfully against the Mau Mau gangs and I shall try and point out some of them.

In the first place, a large part of the country in which Mau Mau operates is without proper roads, and, of course, a part of it is actual forest on the mountain slopes of Mount Kenya and the Aberdares. Communication systems are very bad and the area is vast. It is not at all easy, therefore, to get the news of the movements of a Mau Mau gang back to a point where there is a Guard Post, a Police Post, or a Military Camp, in time for the Security Forces to get into action before the gang that was the subject of the report has melted away.

Moving across country on foot, up and down steep hillsides—which even jeeps and land-rovers cannot negotiate —it is relatively easy for a gang to take evasive action from mechanical patrols. Foot patrols, on the security side, consist in a large part of personnel—both British and African—who are not really familiar with the terrain, and who therefore have to have guides drawn from among the local people, such as the Home Guards. But a guided party that is trying to follow a trail can never move so fast as a group of people who all know the district and who can scatter to meet again at a prearranged rendezvous, without any fear of getting lost. For the Security Forces who are trying to follow a gang, the risk of scattering is great. Individuals who get isolated from their group can so easily get lost, or be ambushed and eliminated without noise, by being slashed to death with a panga.

Another immense handicap of the Security Forces, is that all over the country there are Kikuyu who, whilst not actually siding with the Mau Mau, are still sufficiently sympathetic with them to give warning of approaching Security Forces, and the speed with which such warnings can be shouted across the valleys is quite astonishing.

Quite apart from this sort of impromptu warning, the Mau Mau organisation is such that in every area there are members—often ostensibly working on the 'loyalists'' side and with strict instructions to do nothing that might make them suspect—whose only duty is to watch for the approach of security patrols whether of the Home Guards, the Police, or the Army, and pass on the news quickly.

Even when such warnings are given by shouting, they can still be made to appear quite harmless by using simple code words. It is so much a normal custom to call out ordinary messages and greetings across the valleys that it is a simple matter for someone, when passing on a warning message, to call across to a friend something like this: 'Njoroge, Njoroge, I am not going to come over this evening' or 'Kamau, I'll come and talk about buying that goat tomorrow.' Owing to prearranged plans Njoroge or Kamau will know that this really means 'There is a patrol coming up from Fort Hall and heading up the valley', and they, in their turn, pass on the message in whatever code they have arranged with the next person in the link-up.

Another big handicap of the Security Forces is the relatively few people in the Police Force or the Army who can speak the Kikuyu language, so that they have to act through the medium of interpreters, who are not always reliable or expert. To be able to interpret well requires that the person doing the job shall know both languages *really well*, and there are relatively few Kikuyu who can put the niceties of their own language into good English, without losing much of its meaning and vice versa. Swahili, the so-called lingua franca of East Africa, is not nearly as much use as it is often claimed to be, and it is very easy to alter the whole meaning of a message or mutilate a piece of vital information (quite unintentionally) when translating it from either English or Kikuyu into Swahili.

Many of the misunderstandings between the population of Kikuyu country and the Security Forces would be of much less consequence if there was a better linguistic link between the two groups. But Kikuyu is not a language that can be easily or quickly learnt by the White Man, so that it is not much use crying over spilt milk now.

Another very grave handicap of the Security Forces lies in the fact that a high proportion of those who are now employed in Security work are not fully trained personnel. This, of course, is inevitable, since the Emergency came very suddenly and people had to be called up and put into important posts, with the barest minimum of training for the tasks they had to undertake. The surprising thing, really, is how well they have succeeded when so many, and so much more serious, blunders might have occurred.

Of course there have been 'incidents' of an unpleasant character; some due to lack of training, some due to insufficiently careful selection of personnel. These incidents attract a wholly undue amount of publicity in the popular overseas press, which seldom takes the trouble to point out that for every such unpleasant incident which comes to light there are tens of thousands of cases where persons, similarly placed, have acted with complete correctitude.

It would be silly to deny that some things have been done, by certain people in the Security Forces, which are utterly disgusting and unworthy of the traditions of the British. These acts are rightly censured and are punished whenever they can be proved. But when they are blazoned in the press, they give a wholly false idea of the attitude and behaviour of the vast majority of the members of the Security Forces.

People who denounce all the Security Forces who are working against the Mau Mau, and who suggest that they are brutal and unjust in their methods, would hardly like it if they and their friends and colleagues were all branded as gunmen and thugs and spivs, just because London harbours people of this kind, whose actions *also* attract much press attention. I think that most will agree that a stranger casually reading about incidents in London in the daily press could easily obtain a very wrong idea of what the behaviour of, shall we say, the ordinary Londoner was like!

A very vexed problem in connection with the work of the Security Forces is that connected with the role played by the R.A.F. There is no doubt at all that small planes used for 'spotting' the movement of gangs and searching for signs of camps high up in the mountains, are of the greatest value, and have more than justified the expense involved. There is, however, a very considerable body of opinion that does not believe that the expenditure involved in using heavy bombers is justified. When bombing was first started it certainly had a psychological effect—for a short time, but this effect wore off relatively soon. The gangs, so far as I know, very soon discovered that in heavily forested country the bombs did more damage to the trees than to personnel. Moreover, when, as in the present case, the 'enemy' is seldom, if ever, to be found in large concentrations and has no big supply bases or transport centres, the material damage done to the enemy by bombing can never be very great and it is doubtful if it is ever commensurate with the cost that is involved. I fully share the view of those who believe that the money at present being used in connection with most of the R.A.F. operations against Mau Mau, could be much more usefully employed in the very costly schemes that must be set up to deal with reconstruction and rehabilitation, during the process of 'winning the peace'.

One of the most difficult and complex tasks of the Security Forces is that which is usually referred to as 'Screening Operations', the most extensive and ambitious of which was the so-called 'Operation Anvil' in which thousands of Kikuyu, Embu, and Meru living in Nairobi were picked up and a large proportion of them kept in temporary detention for further screening.

People living outside Kenya often find it very difficult to understand why such screening operations should be in any way necessary. In Nairobi and, to a less extent, in other towns, the Mau Mau organisation was always very active and it would not be wrong to say that, to a considerable extent, the headquarters of Mau Mau were in Nairobi, with a vast network of supporters scattered throughout the city. There is no outward sign by which one can tell whether a man is a Mau Mau supporter or not, for the original practice of making seven cuts on those who were 'initiated' into the movement was very quickly abandoned, because it made recognition by the police too easy.

As I have tried to show in earlier chapters, a vast number of Mau Mau adherents are occupied in normal everyday occupations in the towns, as house servants, office boys, clerks, car drivers, etc. These people, acting on very definite instructions, behave towards the Europeans in a manner which suggests that they are anti-Mau Mau. On them lies the burden of finding out where arms and ammunition can be obtained and the collecting of information as already outlined.

Even when such people are known to 'loyalist' Kikuyu living in the towns to be Mau Mau followers, it is not easy for these people to give evidence against them or point them out. If they did so, swift retaliation would follow. But once they have been picked up during a screening operation, they can often be identified by the special screening teams and, in this way, dealt with with very much less risk that retaliation will follow against those who identified them.

Moreover, Mau Mau headquarters had evolved a most complex system of forged passes, forged identity cards, and other papers, so that many full-time Mau Mau operators were able to remain in Nairobi, ostensibly employed by respectable firms and apparently going about their lawful occasions. When a screening operation is carried out and every inhabitant of a given part of the city has his papers checked, it is *not* possible to pick out those with forged papers and credentials in a hurry. To do this properly involves a most complex checking system against the filed documents which accompany the issue of all such genuine papers.

In a screening operation, therefore, all those about whom there is any doubt at all, have to be held whilst their credentials can be carefully checked. They also pass in front of the 'screening teams' who very often can identify persons who have been 'wanted' for many months.

There is no doubt that screening operations do cause a great deal of real inconvenience to genuine loyal Africans, but this is a part of the price that has to be paid for the task of breaking Mau Mau. It is, in fact, most remarkable how the real 'loyalists', who have been put to great inconveniences again and again during screening operations, cheerfully accept the inconveniences they have to suffer.

It is often asked, and not unreasonably, why a person who has been screened once cannot be given some document to show that he has been screened and cleared, in order to save him from having to undergo a similar experience in the future; often in the near future.

The answer is, of course, that no document that was given, in this way, to a person who had been cleared would be really safe. The Mau Mau planners, if such documents existed, would very quickly acquire some by force and, after suitable forging and alterations, issue them to their own people. They would also probably produce skilled copies for issue, as required, to their agents.

The screening operations have done immense good— especially in Nairobi—although, despite all the precautions taken, a number of leading Mau Mau were still able to escape the net, while many innocent people suffered temporary hardships. Here again, if a far greater number of European personnel with a good knowledge of the vernacular languages had been available and more fully trained police, much time could have been saved, and less inconvenience caused to innocent people.

There has been a good deal of ill-informed comment in some circles in England in connection with proceedings in the Kenya Courts against the Mau Mau offenders. It is by no means always realised how great the difficulties are which have to be overcome by those preparing cases for trial before the Courts. Nor is there an adequate appreciation of the care which is taken to prevent any injustice.

Criticism is of two extreme kinds. On the one hand one hears people say, 'Why could not the Police bring better evidence than they did, in such and such a case, and secure a conviction?' 'Surely other witnesses must have been available?' On the other extreme are those who consider that the evidence against some of those who are convicted is too slender and that a proportion of those who have been convicted should have been released, or even never brought before the Courts at all.

There are also people who criticise—often most unfairly —when Government executes a Detention Order under the Emergency Regulations, against a person who has been acquitted by a Court.

All these three aspects of the problems which the Courts of Justice have to deal with therefore deserve our careful attention.

Let us first of all look at the difficulties of the Police when trying to get together sufficient evidence of an offence, committed by a Mau Mau terrorist, to bring him to justice. Information is probably received, in the first place, from what are often called 'informers' (or else from definite secret agents that have been placed inside the Movement), that X is a gunman who often carries an illegal fire-arm and who has committed a series of murders in, shall we say, the locality of Nairobi. The information comes from first one and then another source, and a description of some sort of the man is obtained as well as a name. The name, however, is almost certainly not his real name, nor even the name on his identity papers, but is probably merely one of several nicknames or aliases under which he passes.

All the information is carded, patrols are given the details, and a watch is kept for a man answering the description. Several 'possibles' probably get picked up and, after checking, released, and in the meantime other agents are set to work to get further information.

Eventually, 'acting on information received', the Police may succeed in picking up the man they want, but unless at the time of his arrest he is carrying an illegal weapon, or ammunition, or is breaking the law in some other way, it is impossible to bring him before a Court.

This could only be done by producing, as witnesses, some of those who have given information about him—the informers and the special intelligence agents, but their identity must be kept secret because of other work which they are doing.

In such cases, if the information is known to be good, and has come from a sufficiently large number of different reliable sources, an application is made for a detention order, since once apprehended, it would clearly be unwise to release a known murderer or gunman, and let him continue his activities during a State of Emergency.

Again and again shooting and murders take place in daylight and in the presence of many people, but before the Police can arrive on the scene, those who have witnessed what has happened melt away and refuse to come forward to offer evidence.

It is easy enough to be severely critical of citizens who, having witnessed a murder of this sort, refuse to come forward to give evidence, but it is not wholly surprising that they do refuse. In cases of ordinary murder, witnesses are almost always willing to come forward, but if a person volunteers to give evidence against a Mau Mau gunman or strangler, he knows, that by doing so, he will at once put his own life and that of his family in danger.

Mau Mau have their agents and spies everywhere and the moment a citizen is known to have made a statement to the Police about a shooting incident, or to have given evidence that may bring a gunman before the Courts, the organisation gets busy and the person concerned is either quietly murdered, or is so threatened together with his family, that he quickly disappears and is unavailable when he is wanted as a witness in Court.

It might be thought that in such circumstances protection could be given to those who offer to give evidence, and, in fact, this is always offered. But the mere fact of providing protection to a potential witness in a Mau Mau case, will not save his family from the retribution of the gangsters, and it is clearly not practicable to give 'protective custody' to every member of a potential witness's family.

Even where sufficiently good evidence has been collected by the Police to bring a Mau Mau gunman or murderer before the Courts, it all too frequently happens that the witnesses change their story when the case is being heard. Sometimes this is due to the man having been intimidated and threatened by the Mau Mau intelligence service. Sometimes it may be because an interpreter, who is pro-Mau Mau, has just sufficiently altered the sense of the questions put to the witness by Counsel, to make his replies in evidence lose their value.

The Courts, after all, can only give their verdict on the actual evidence before them. It therefore often happens that persons whom the Police know, for certain, have committed foul murders, get acquitted. Naturally this also happens sometimes in connection with ordinary murder trials anywhere in the world. Under a State of Emergency, however, and when dealing with organised gunmen, a Court acquittal cannot always be allowed to result in the complete release of the man to go and commit more crimes of violence. It therefore sometimes becomes necessary to detain a man under the Emergency Regulations when he has been acquitted by a Court. People who do not know the full inside story may think this is unfair, but it is only done when it is absolutely necessary.

In England, I have heard many suggestions that justice is no longer done in Kenya today.

It is assumed by critics outside Kenya that many innocent people are sentenced by the Courts when they are dealing with Mau Mau cases. I would say rather that the Courts are so careful (and rightly so) that the reverse is often the case. I do not think that Kenya justice is any more likely to result in a sentence on an innocent man than the processes of justice anywhere else. The Magistrates and Judges are so careful not to convict on inadequate evidence that, in present-day conditions, numbers of Mau Mau are acquitted who are undoubtedly guilty.

If some of these people are subsequently detained under Detention Orders, that is not necessarily unjust, for this course is only taken when the available evidence (even if it could not be produced in Court) is such that the Governor, or a senior officer to whom he has deputed his powers, is wholly satisfied that it is necessary in the interests of law and order and public safety.

XI

WHAT MUST BE DONE: RELIGIOUS, EDUCATIONAL, AND ECONOMIC REFORMS

Mau Mau is losing. Even if the actual fighting against the hard core continues for many months or even years to come, even if the terrorists murder many more loyal Kikuyu and European women and children, the masses of the people know that Mau Mau has failed them, both as a political movement aimed to drive out the White Man and win self-government, and as a religion.

The Kikuyu themselves no longer believe that the *methods* of Mau Mau can achieve anything for them, but that does not mean that they do not still support many of the Mau Mau aims.

Unquestionably there were genuine grievances, upon which Mau Mau leaders built up their whole propaganda programme. These must be removed. The vast majority of the Kíkuyu people had very certainly drifted into a state of mental unstability and irresponsibility, and were thus an easy prey to Mau Mau religion and hysteria. Steps must be taken to rectify this.

What has happened in recent years among the Kikuyu people—because they happened to be the tribe psychologically most ready to fall an easy prey to false propaganda— could easily happen in the next ten or twenty years in other tribes in East Africa, UNLESS those in authority are prepared to recognise frankly that they made many mistakes, and unless they are prepared to spend considerable sums of money in the very near future in rectifying those errors.

The cost of the things that must be done, if any success in 'winning the peace' is to be achieved, will be immense, *but not nearly so great* as would be the cost of having to deal with another outbreak, such as Mau Mau, in the future.

As the result of the recent constitutional changes in Kenya, the European, Asian, and African leaders now have the chance, jointly, to plan wisely, to act courageously, and to achieve in Kenya a state of inter-racial harmony and co-operation such as is yet unknown in the African Continent.

There will be much opposition from 'die-hards', there will be bitter criticism on the one hand that too much and on the other hand that too little, is being done. But if wise leaders can be found who have both courage and vision, who are sincere and convincing, success can be achieved.

It is not only in the field of political leadership that these qualities will be required. They will also be needed, vitally necessary in fact, in the religious leaders as well as in the field of education, in all its aspects.

The Kikuyu (and all the other tribes in Kenya) are people who need a simple, deep-rooted faith, a religion that is alive and real.

Most of the East African tribes, and particularly so the group which includes the Kikuyu, Embu, and Kamba, had a religion very like that of the Old Testament. They worshipped a Supreme God—not wooden idols or graven images—a God who required blood sacrifices, but who also answered sincere prayer and liked to be thanked for his mercies.

Many of the customs which went hand in hand with religion were also very similar to those of Old Testament times: polygamy was approved of, a widow lived with her deceased husband's brother and by him continued to have children; circumcision was practised. Many of the forbidden things of the Pentateuch were among the taboos of the tribes, as, for example, the ban on eating the meat of any animal that did not have a cloven hoof.

The coming of the European, with his new religion of

Christianity, had the effect, inevitably, of making hundreds of thousands turn away from the religion of their fathers and seek the religion of the newcomers.

The Missionaries came to bring the Christian faith to these people, but they came from many different sects, each with its own version of Christianity, and most of them were not content simply to lead the people out of the Old Testament into the New. They tried, instead, to skip a stage and leap straight from the Old Testament to the formal worship of the twentieth-century churches of Western Europe.

While it is certainly a part of the doctrine of the Church of England that a Christian may not have more than one wife, it is equally certain, as I see it, that that is not one of the fundamental teachings of Christ Himself, or of the Apostles.

The practice of 'female circumcision' is also not one of the customs that go with the teaching of the Church of England, but there is no reason to believe that Christ would have regarded it as sinful. The fact that in some cases the surgical operation was so unskilfully performed as to cause physical danger to a woman in childbirth, was surely no justification for attacking the custom as un-Christian, rather than attacking the lack of skill, and the way in which the operation was sometimes done.

Yet the Missionaries, who came to bring the Gospel of Christ to a people who were very ready to receive it, insisted that polygamy was a bar to full membership of the Church; was, in fact, sinful. At a later date, many of the Missions tried to make a renunciation of the custom of female circumcision a condition of full Church membership. They also frowned on those widows who, in accordance with Bible practice and their own tribal customs, allowed the brothers of their deceased husbands to sleep with them and beget children by them. This was adultery, they said; but was it?

Very many Kikuyu and other Africans have turned away from Christianity, not because they did not believe in the teachings of the Master, not because they did not feel a need for the faith which they found in Him, but simply because they could not accept as necessary to their belief so many of the things that the different Mission Church organisations insisted upon.

Church leaders today must make up their minds as to whether they prefer to be loyal to the doctrine of Churches and the teachings of the 'Early Fathers', or whether they will be loyal *only* to the teaching of Christ Himself, and the New Testament.

If they try to confuse the fundamental teachings of the New Testament with things that are nothing more than British social custom, or doctrines laid down by men, whose wisdom is at least open to some doubt, they will not succeed in winning the masses of the Africans to real Christianity. If they fail to do this, then assuredly other religions will be taken up, religions like Mau Mauism or Communism (for that, too, is a sort of religion).

If the existing Missionary organisations, the many Christian Churches—whether of the Established Church or Nonconformist—which at present work in Africa, are not prepared to make a new approach, then something else must be done.

I consider that sincere Africans who want to follow the teachings of Christ, but who do not wish to be bound by the rules of the Churches, but only those of the Bible, ought to be encouraged to start Independent African Churches which would have to be both helped and guided. They would have to be as welcome in the councils of the United African Churches as all the other sects. The Church of England pastors do not refuse to help the Presbyterians or the Methodists. The Seventh Day Adventists share in the councils of the United Christian Churches of Kenya. Why should the African Independent Churches not be equally treated, provided they abide by the teachings of Christ and the New Testament, and even if they reject some of the Church's later laws.

If the Kikuyu Independent Pentecostal Church and the Kikuyu African Orthodox Church had been helped and advised, instead of being shunned and attacked, Mau Mau as a religion could never have obtained the hold it did.

When the K.C.A. was a purely political movement, it was unable to get the support of more than some ten thousand people, but once it changed over and became the Mau Mau religion it drew hundreds of thousands, *who are now, however, rejecting it because it has failed them.* The followers of Mau Mau religion would probably never have gone over to it if the Independent Churches had been helped and guided and had remained true to the teachings of Christ, while at the same time allowing polygamy, female circumcision, and the practice of widows raising up children by their deceased husband's brothers, even though the latter were already married. As it was, because they received no help, because they were openly accused of 'not being Christian at all', they threw over Christ and in His place substituted Jomo Kenyatta, who believed neither in the Ten Commandments nor the precepts of the Sermon on the Mount.

If the breakdown of the old religion of the Kikuyu and the failure of twentieth-century Western Christianity to take its place (because it went too far beyond the simple teachings of the New Testament) is one of the causes of Mau Mau, so also is the failure of the education system.

Vast sums of money have been spent, both by the Missionary organisations and by Government, on secular education for the Africans, on the teaching of the three R's in the host of elementary schools, and upon more advanced subjects in the primary and secondary schools.

Provision for such education was most necessary and the facilities, at present available, are still all too inadequate for the hundreds of thousands of African children who want it. But the education that was provided did not go nearly far enough, because it took little or no account of the fact that once the African children started to become literate they would no longer be willing to listen to the advice and teaching of their parents and the elders of the tribe. These were the people who in olden days trained the young to grow up into reasonable, responsible members of adult society.

In olden days, as I showed in my earlier book, young boys and girls learnt the laws of the tribe, the rules of behaviour, and the principles of honesty, respect for authority and responsibility, from the tribal elders. Stealing, murder, drunkenness, adultery, dishonesty, disrespect for authority, were all stigmatised as things which must not have any place in adult life. A youth who showed signs of not accepting these rules could be held back from initiation year after year. He was not fit to be an adult. Moreover, he was the laughing-stock of the people of his own age.

As our modern education system taught the young to read and write, so did it, also, create a feeling of disrespect for the illiterate elders. More and even more the young refused to listen or to learn and take advice. In those schools where they were in direct contact with a European Missionary—and especially in the early days when there were fewer pupils to contend with—the Missionaries did include education in these things as part of the instruction that was given to the pupils. But, more and more, it became necessary to leave the bulk of the teaching in the schools to African teachers, very many of whom were young and not too competent, and who felt that it was not for them to try and usurp the duties of the Elders. Anyway, they were being paid to teach in the book-learning sense, and the time-table was usually fully taken up with this work and left little or no time for anything else.

This was especially true in the elementary and bush schools, which in fact were the places where instruction in morals and good behaviour, etc., were the most important.

The salary scales of teachers were also very low and, in consequence, the people who were attracted to this profession were not always the best, but quite often those who could not obtain better-paid employment elsewhere.

Many boys and girls thus grew up into young men and women, having some little book-learning, but without any real training in how to behave as adults in the life of the community. Dishonesty of all kinds became common and sexual morals degenerated. The old sexual laws were no longer obeyed (they were not even known), but there were no others that had been inculcated in the young. Drunkenness and disrespect for authority became widespread.

The blame for all this must, to a large extent, rest upon the Europeans, for we failed to appreciate the demoralising effect of a little book-learning, if it was not accompanied by very careful instruction in moral behaviour and in citizenship.

Thus there came into existence a huge body of youth who were not only without any real religion, but who were also without moral principles, and who had had no character training to speak of. It is hardly surprising that they fell to the eloquence of Mau Mau oratory and degenerated into gunmen and gangsters.

A complete overhaul of our educational system is needed, not only as it affects the Kikuyu, but also all the other tribes.

In the first place, there must be a very, very, much more careful training of teachers, and on a much more extensive scale. The candidates for such training must be very carefully selected in the first place. The greatest possible effort must be made in respect of those teachers who are destined to work in bush and elementary schools, although the training for teachers in the primary and secondary schools must not be neglected. The teachers must learn not only how to teach the ordinary school curriculum subjects, but how to guide and mould the character of their pupils.

The necessity for training the young in preparation for adult life and its responsibilities was fully recognised by tribal custom, at a time when the adult only had to be prepared to take part in the relatively simple life of the tribal community. Now the adult African has got to live *in a very complex multi-racial society*, and for this reason the need for careful training and preparation is far greater, while in fact there is much less of it.

Considerable sums of money will be needed, but if vast sums can be found to quell Mau Mau, surely similar or even greater sums can be found to forestall similar outbreaks in the future?

Turning next to the economic problems of 'winning the peace', there can be no doubt whatever of the importance, in the minds of the people, of the land problem. This I have attempted to stress in the chapter dealing with propaganda methods. Today, in the Kikuyu Land Unit, the population density is such that it is quite impossible for the average peasant to grow enough for his legitimate needs, on the land available to him. It has become necessary today not only to grow the actual food requirements of the family, but also a sufficient surplus which, when sold, can provide the money to pay for such other necessities as clothes, blankets, cooking utensils, fuel, foodstuffs such as tea and sugar, and also for children's school fees, taxes, etc.

It is often claimed that if the land that is already available were better farmed, it would be sufficient. This is not wholly true. There are considerable parts of Kikuyu country which are so steep that they ought not to carry cultivation at all. Nevertheless, some measure of relief would certainly be brought about by improvements in agricultural methods. It is most essential, however, that in this respect we should 'make haste slowly'. As I pointed out in an earlier book of mine,[1] the increase in soil erosion in Kikuyu country was in large measure due to the British advocating methods of cultivation which were not suitable to the light friable soils and steep slopes of Kikuyu country. Their old system, arrived at by empirical methods, was far more satisfactory, at least from the point of view of soil protection.

Whereas it may well prove necessary to find some additional land for a part of the huge Kikuyu peasant population, I do not think that the main answer to land overcrowding is to be found along these lines.

Today, many Kikuyu are urban workers, employed in many different capacities in towns and cities. These people have no alternative, under existing circumstances, but to retain a piece of land in the Native Land Unit. They thus live dual lives, as urban workers and yet with peasant holdings.

There are a variety of reasons for this. In the first place, the average accommodation for urban African labour is so inadequate that it is almost impossible for a man to have his wife and family with him. Although there are some cottages available for the better-paid urban workers, the majority live either in small single rooms, usually about 10 ft. by 6 ft., or worse still, have as their 'home' a mere 'bed space' 8 ft. by 4 ft., in a room shared by two others with similar 'bed spaces'.

Obviously these very small single rooms and these 'bed spaces' can never become a real home for a man and his wife and family. Consequently, most urban workers keep a hold on their little piece of land in the Native Land Unit and it is there that the worker's wife and family live. They thus live most of the time at a great distance from the head of the family, and they also depend, to a very considerable extent, upon what they can grow on their land themselves for their means of livelihood.

[1] *Kenya Contrasts and Problems.*

For the lower-paid urban African workers, the salary scale is such that it would be quite impossible to support a wife and family on it, and it is often hard enough for the men to keep out of debt while only feeding, clothing, and housing themselves. Thus, in reality, much of the work done by urban Africans is subject to a sort of 'hidden subsidy', paid, not by the State or by the employer, but ironically by the employee! It is scarcely surprising that the urban Africans, living under such conditions, have been among the most ardent supporters of Mau Mau, with its promise of Utopia to come.

If the very serious overcrowding of the Kikuyu (and some other) Native Land Units is to be remedied, a great deal could be achieved by a revolutionary change in urban African housing provision. If an urban worker could have accommodation which was adequate for himself and his wife and family, so that he felt he had a real urban home, he would, in many cases, gladly give up the plot which he has retained in the Reserve and thus make more land available to the true peasants. If this improvement is to be achieved TWO other conditions would also have to be fulfilled. The rates of pay would have to be so up-graded that a man could genuinely provide for his wife and family's needs, *from his own pay*, since they could no longer depend for even part of their livelihood from the produce of the land. Secondly, it would have to be possible for a man (if he so wished) to acquire the ownership of his cottage or flat, perhaps by some sort of purchase by instalment system.

At present the urban worker goes on paying rent, month after month, from his meagre earnings, and, at the end, has nothing. When, therefore, his working days are done, or if he becomes seriously ill and loses his job, he is homeless.

Provided that a genuine solution can be found to this problem of the urban Africans, whereby they can become fully urban (and contentedly so), then a very great step in the right direction will have been achieved. Any money so spent will, at one and the same time, have helped to solve two problems. It will remove the real grievances of the urban workers, thereby making them less likely to fall a prey to subversive agitators, while at the same time it will have done much to make more land available to the true peasants without adding any new land to the Native Land Units.

Something in the nature of an old age pension scheme, and a sickness insurance, will also need to be worked out and put into effect for the urban Africans, if they are to become truly urban. This will require careful planning and will be costly, but it is rapidly becoming essential.

In this connection it must be noted that there is a widespread view, among European employers of labour in Kenya, that the African labourer is not worth more than the very low rate of wages which he now receives 'because it takes four Africans to do the work of one European on the same job'. This statement is open to challenge. There are Africans who are working as firemen and engine-drivers and chauffeurs, who seem to be fully as competent as many white men on corresponding work, but drawing less pay. But, even if the premise were wholly true, it still remains also true that few Africans get even a quarter of the rates of pay for a comparable grade of European labour.

There have been big increases in African salary scales during the last few years, as well as in 'Cost of Living Allowances', but these have not really kept pace with the rise in cost of some of the basic requirements of the African, as for example, maize flour. Maize—one of the staple foods of many Africans—has risen in price from about 6s. a bag to 56s. a bag. Meat has risen to about five times its earlier price, while many other foodstuffs have had similar rises, but the wages increase is proportionately not nearly so great, so that a labourer who now draws perhaps 100s. *a month*, is much worse off than he was seven years ago when he was only drawing 45s.

It is true that the average African worker in the towns does not really put in a full day's hard work. Many of them, because of their low rate of pay, start work in the morning on nothing but a cup of tea and perhaps have another cup of tea and a bun for lunch. They can only afford one proper meal a day, and they have that in the evening. When in addition to this low calory diet the individual is also not really physically fit, due to being infected with internal parasites, or because he suffers from an enlarged spleen caused by malaria, it is hardly to be expected that he can put in really hard work for many hours a day.

I am convinced that properly fed, in proper health, and with sufficient incentive, the African can do just as good a day's work as any comparable European labourer, but at present these prerequisites are all missing. We tend to put the cart before the horse. If we can improve the health and the diet of the African labourer and give him a greater incentive to good work, he will do it and justify the greater cost that would be entailed, and the higher rates of pay he would then earn.

Another major problem that must be solved, if peace and prosperity are to return to Kenya, is that which is connected with agricultural labour in the 'White Highlands', on European-owned farms.

At present, the Kikuyu agricultural workers who form the great bulk of the farm labour, are, in most cases, drawn from what are called 'squatters'. The squatter system has been in existence for a long time, but it is not fully understood in Great Britain, because of the different connotation of the word 'squatter' in the English mind.

A 'squatter' in Kenya is an African who enters into a 'squatter contract' with a European farm-owner, whereby he has the right to come and live on the farm, with his family, and is given the permission to cultivate a certain limited acreage and, perhaps, keep some livestock. In return for this, he undertakes to work for the farmer for so many days a year, and his adult sons, if they remain on the farm, must do likewise. The wage scale for squatters is very low indeed—at any rate, for those who do ordinary unskilled manual labour—but this is compensated for by the fact that the squatter and his family can usually earn a very reasonable income from the sale of crops grown on the land which they are permitted to cultivate.

Relations between farmer and squatter are, in the majority of cases, excellent and, until recently, the squatter labourer was usually a very contented person. But District Councils and other bodies began to insist on a reduction in the acreage allowed to squatter families in the White Highlands. Increasingly restrictive measures were introduced governing the number of stock a squatter could own, while there was little or no corresponding increase in the wages paid. Dissention appeared, and many squatters felt that their position was being made intolerable.

More serious was the fact that every squatter always had the nagging fear that something might happen which would result in a termination of his squatter contract. Perhaps the farmer, with whom he had been on the best of terms for many years, would die and the farm be sold to someone who did not want squatters. He would·be told to leave. Possibly the owner would decide to sell up, and move elsewhere. Always there was the uncertainty about the future, and the squatter well knew that, after being settled with his family and his stock on one farm for many years, it might prove very different indeed to find a new place to go to, especially as the demand for squatter labour was declining, with the increasing mechanisation of agricultural methods in Kenya.

In my opinion, the squatter system is a most unsatisfactory one and, certainly, the Mau Mau leaders were able to get a very big following among these people, because of their discontent and mental state of uncertainty.

There will always be a need for agricultural labour on the European farms, and there will always be European farms upon which much of the economy and progress of the whole country (including the progress of the African) depends. The squatter system will, I think, have to be abandoned altogether, and be replaced by something wholly different.

I believe that it will be necessary and desirable to set aside land, all over the European farming area, for small African villages. In these villages the African labourer could either own, or else rent, a cottage with a small cottage garden, something that he could regard as a real home. If a man lost his job on one farm, he would still have a home to live in while looking for other employment. If he choose to move to a different area, he could dispose of his cottage and acquire one in another village. From this village the labourers would go out to work on foot, by bicycle, or by bus (according to the distance), to work on farms within reach of their particular village and return at night.

Naturally, since such a labourer would no longer have some of his employer's land to cultivate and to bring him in an income, he would have to be paid a much higher rate of pay, while he, on his part, would have to work sufficiently hard to earn that higher pay. In such villages, as I foresee them, there would be a village school, a cottage hospital or perhaps dispensary, and a little village church or other place of worship, shops, a community centre, and a village policeman. The latter would be based on the English pattern and would be a person who knew each and all of his people in the village and was as much their friend and helper as he was the arm of the law.

All this would mean untold advantages when compared with the present position of the squatters. It would, however, mean certain basic changes in the present 'White Highland' policy, since Africans would be allowed to own land and property in these villages.

Naturally, the full details of any such scheme would

need careful working out, and one or two 'pilot villages' would have to be established as a start, to test the practicability of the idea, and to learn how to organise such a village for the best advantage of both the workers and the employers. Nevertheless, I feel sure that a solution along these lines must come, and come soon, and the squatter system must be abandoned.

XII

WHAT MUST BE DONE:
SOCIAL AND POLITICAL REFORMS

In the last chapter I indicated that while it was true that
the pressure on land in the Kikuyu Native Land Unit had
provided one of the genuine grievances, which had made
it possible for Mau Mau propaganda to succeed, the
remedy did not lie solely in finding more land for the tribe,
but in doing certain other things which would have the
effect of easing the pressure.

There is another aspect of this same problem which is
social rather than economic, and yet has a major bearing
on the economic aspect.

The increase in Kikuyu population over the past fifty
years has been phenomenal. This has been due to a number
of causes and is one of the principal reasons why the
pressure on the land is now so great. In the olden days,
Kikuyu law did not allow a woman to have a child more
than once in three years, and if you asked an Elder why this
law was made, he would reply, 'Because if she did, the child
she was nursing and the child in her womb would both
suffer, and the woman would suffer too'. In order to obey
this rule of spaced births the Kikuyu women did not abstain
from sex life after the birth of a baby, but practised a form
of birth control which seems to have been very effective.
The only conditions under which this rule was relaxed
was when a baby died in infancy, and then a woman
would take all possible steps to have another baby as soon
as possible.

This rule of spaced birth had the effect of slowing down
the birth rate, while, in addition, the rate of infant mortality
between birth and about the age of six or seven was so

high that population increase was fairly slow. Moreover, the oft-recurring epidemics of smallpox and other death-dealing diseases kept down the rate of population increase still further.

With the coming of the European civilisation, everything has changed. The law governing the spacing of births has been abandoned by the vast majority of the tribe and more especially by those who have been linked in any way with the Missions, so that most women now have babies at far more frequent intervals. But in addition to the far greater number of babies born there has also been a huge reduction in the infant death rate, owing to the introduction of modern medical facilities, hospitals, etc., and the teaching of hygiene. Moreover, the Medical Department has succeeded in reducing epidemics to such a degree that the overall death rate has also been drastically reduced, and the expectancy of life increased.

All this has meant that the rate of population increase is now alarmingly great, and, if it continues at its present rate, will seriously threaten the economy of the Kikuyu Land Units in the very near future.

In the olden days—subject always to the wise rule governing the spacing of births—the Kikuyu liked to have as many children as possible. The economic unit was the extended family and the more there were the more could be achieved. But, today, that too has changed. There has been a major swing away from the 'extended family'[1] to the small individual family, in our Western European sense.

The change in the whole economic structure, too, and the vast number of new needs of the people, means that if a man has too big a family he cannot possibly hope to feed them, clothe them, house them, and give them education.

[1] By the 'extended family' I mean the old Kikuyu conception that all of the man's first cousins ranked as his brothers and their children as his children, and he had the same responsibilites to all these people, as to his own brothers and their children. See p. 32 of my earlier book for details.

Hundreds of the more educated Kikuyu and other Africans in Kenya are now, therefore, beginning to seek advice from the Europeans about methods of family limitation. Many of my more educated Kikuyu friends would like to limit their family to three or four children only, whereas, in point of fact, they find themselves burdened with eight or nine.

Unfortunately it is true that the methods of birth control which are now so widely and successfully used by many Europeans, are not really satisfactory for the African. Either they are too expensive for him at his present economic level, or they involve processes such as douching which are not really possible in homes without proper water supplies, and with water which is often most impure. There is, in fact, a most urgent need for science to treat the problem of finding satisfactory methods of birth control for peasant communities, as one of extreme urgency.

This is not only a Kikuyu or a Kenya problem, it is one which faces all Africa, India, and China to an equal degree.

No solutions to the other problems dealt with in this book will by themselves suffice, if this problem, which is so closely connected with population increase and pressure on the land, is not boldly tackled. Under no circumstances must birth control be urged upon the African, but when he asks for it, we must be in a position to give him something really suitable and satisfactory. And let it be noted that he is already beginning to ask for it, so the matter is one of urgency. Many Kikuyu, today, openly say they would prefer a small family that they could feed, clothe, house, and educate properly, than a large one that has to exist as paupers.

I believe that Government must take steps to initiate serious research into this problem, for surely, if tackled seriously, it is not beyond science to find a suitable answer, and so make it possible for the peasant family to aim at quality rather than quantity in his offspring.

There is also a most urgent need to study ways and means of próviding suitable work for Kikuyu, and other African, girls, which they can undertake after schooling is over and before marriage (or in the case of some, instead of marriage). This problem is far more acute in the towns than among the peasant communities—where the girls of this age find plenty to do helping their parents on the land. In the towns, there is almost nothing for the teenage girls to do. A few, very few, train as hospital nurses, some become 'ayahs' or children's nurses in European households, but the majority wander about aimlessly, get into trouble and have illegitimate babies long before they marry.

Those who have close knowledge of Mau Mau know, only too well, how many teenage girls in the towns have dropped into membership of the movement and have even become very active members of murder gangs—often out of sheer boredom at having nothing to do all day.

As urbanisation increases, so will the number of such girls in the towns increase, and something must be done, and done urgently, to find a way of training them and giving them useful occupations until they marry.

I can see no reason why, for some of them, the answer should not be domestic service, provided always that they are given suitable accommodation and are reasonably looked after. In Entebbe, Uganda, one finds a certain number of Baganda girls going into domestic service very successfully, and there is no reason why Kenya African girls should not do likewise and thus provide some occupation for town girls after leaving school and before marriage.

More too is needed in the way of girls' clubs and girls' social centres for the young girls in the towns. They are increasing in numbers and will become very much more numerous if better housing for Africans is provided and more of the town workers become truly urban. At present, unmarried girls in the townships are mainly to be found among that small part of the African urban population

145

that has cottage accommodation. The problem already exists for them and, if more true urbanisation takes place, as it must do, it will become much more acute.

Much more too needs to be done for the young African men in the way of welfare work, for working in the towns, with their evenings idle and unoccupied, many fall into evil ways and sooner or later turn to crime. Some community halls do already exist, but much more could be done than has been done so far.

The so-called 'colour bar' is at last beginning to disappear in Kenya. This cannot be achieved by legislation, in spite of all that is sometimes suggested by over-zealous opponents of racial discrimination. The change from a colour bar to a culture bar is a thing that can only happen as a result of more enlightened public opinion and there are signs that this change is beginning to take place.

Full racial co-operation for the benefit of all the Kenya races can obviously never be achieved in the field of politics and economics, so long as a colour bar is maintained.

A real understanding of mutual problems rarely comes from discussions at a conference table, if those who are participating have never visited each other's homes and had any kind of social contact. I believe that the Europeans in Kenya, including at least some of the political leaders, are beginning to realise this and it augurs well for the future.

We have reached a stage in Kenya's history where Kenya-born Europeans who have been to universities in England and elsewhere are returning to take part in the life of the country. These young people have mixed freely on an equal footing with Asian and African students at the universities and their attitude is often a very different one from that of their parents. It is bringing in a healthy and much more realistic outlook to the colour question.

In this connection the use of a common language, English, plays a very large part in breaking down barriers of misunderstanding, and this must have an important bearing, too, upon political problems. At present all too few of the leading African politicians are really fluent in the English language. They speak it to some extent, but their knowledge is, to a greater or lesser degree, incomplete, which makes free and easy discussion with political leaders of other races (European and Asian) much more difficult.

Since it is clearly essential that Africans who are chosen to become members of Legislative Council should understand and speak English, the selection of people for this work is limited to the few who have the linguistic qualifications. There are many outstanding African leaders, men of personality and ability, whose lack of adequate English renders them unable to play a fuller part in working for racial co-operation in the sphere of politics. All too often those who have been overseas and who have a good knowledge of our language are not the ones who would make the best representatives of their people in the Legislative Assembly.

If Kenya is to make greater progress along the path of racial co-operation, I feel that a great many more of her African people must be given the chance to visit England and improve their knowledge of the language, while at the same time broadening their outlook and background.

Before the State of Emergency was declared, there existed in Kenya an inter-tribal political organisation known as the Kenya African Union. This had become so dominated by members of the Kikuyu tribe, that it had gradually been turned into nothing more than a convenient coverage for Mau Mau activities. It was therefore banned.

There is, however, clearly a great need for some such organisation whereby the leading Africans of the different tribes can pool their ideas and exchange opinions on current political problems.

The weakness of the organisation known as the Kenya African Union was that membership was open to any *individual*, of any tribe, who cared to pay his fees and join. It was thus possible for membership, at the lowest level, to be so overweighted by one tribe that the election of office bearers could turn it into more or less a tribal political organisation. It will be essential that some body be formed to take the place of the Kenya African Union. It should, however, be truly representative of all the bigger and more progressive tribes, with no single tribe having any chance of dominating its policies.

All the loyal tribes already have their own political organisations of one kind and another and the central political organisation might well consist of the representatives of the tribal political parties, without any individual membership at all. Political leaders of several tribes with whom I have discussed this question take the line that individual membership is necessary, since it is the subscriptions of individual members which mount up and which make available the funds which such a central political body must have at its disposal.

A reasonable answer to this difficulty will have to be found and advice and guidance will have to be given to any such body, in its early stages, to see that it develops along healthy and useful lines.

When the State of Emergency was declared it became necessary to ban a large number of vernacular newspapers, mostly in the Kikuyu and Kamba languages, because they were being used in a wholly subversive manner to stir up racial hatred. It was unfortunate that this banning of so many papers became necessary, for properly run vernacular newspapers have a very important part to play in the life of the community. The trouble in the past has been that so many of those who have set out to run newspapers for their fellow Africans had no training, whatsoever, in this profession. Moreover, they seldom realised that, in its early days, no newspaper can ever hope to be a paying proposition. That stage only comes when a paper is fully established and has a big enough circulation to attract a reasonable amount of advertising within its pages.

In consequence, it happened, again and again, that an African newspaper owner and editor found himself in financial difficulties. He could then be fairly easily persuaded to accept funds from an organisation like the K.C.A. or Mau Mau in return for his support of the movement and its policy, in his columns.

Very few of the editors ever knew enough about journalism to know the difference between justifiable criticism of Government policy and seditious utterances. Nor did they realise how necessary it is for those who run a newspaper to check the sources of their more sensational stories, before publishing what might prove to be wholly groundless allegations that would get them into trouble.

Now that there are signs that the end of the Emergency may not be too far away, it is clear that much thought must be given to the question of the future of the African press in Kenya. Government-sponsored newspapers run by the African Information Services will never fill the need, for they will always be regarded as merely a part of the Government propaganda machine. Free African newspapers must come back into the field of journalism in Kenya and they must be helped to come back.

In the first place, I feel that would-be editors should be given the opportunity to attend schools of journalism either in England or in Southern Rhodesia (where I believe there is an excellent one) to get a better knowledge of what is required in this profession.

English and other European journalists must be found who will be willing to give guidance and a helping hand. It may even be necessary to find some means of providing finance for African papers (without demanding any *quid pro quo* in the form of a right to control the papers) so long as they abide by the law.

A good newspaper, however critical of Government

policy, can do much to mould public opinion and to educate the people. It can also provide a wonderful outlet for the release of 'hot air' in its correspondence columns.

Government clearly cannot undertake anything to do with reorganising an African vernacular press after the Emergency, for, if it did so, any paper so produced would be regarded as a Government-sponsored organ and would at once fail to fulfil its purpose. There must, therefore, be found men of good will, either in Kenya or outside, who believe that this problem is one of real urgency for the future of East Africa and who will be willing to do something concrete to help African newspapers to get re-established on a better footing than existed before, and with editors who have had, at least, some training and also, if possible, apprenticeship in journalism, elsewhere.

Finally, in the field of politics it is essential to consider how the African population of Kenya can be made to feel that they have a more real say in the affairs of the country. The recent reorganisation of Government under the 'Lyttelton Plan' has resulted in one African Minister and one or two Under-Secretaries, and there are also rather more African representatives in Legislative Council than there used to be. Nevertheless, the Africans feel that they are not truly represented at all, for the African members of Council were not elected by the people, but chosen by Government from names submitted through various African Councils, but without their having the final say in the choice of their representatives.

The time has clearly come when some modifications must be made. Even if the Africans were to elect, as their representatives to Council, persons whom Government did not approve of, it would at least mean that the masses could no longer legitimately claim that there was no one who really represented them, and who really knew their views.

Elections for the next Legislative Council should take

place in 1956. I believe that all the bigger Kenya tribes should be allowed to choose their own representatives—by election—although the detailed way in which the elections would be carried out would have to be a matter of careful thought.

So far as the Kikuyu, Embu, Meru tribes are concerned I think that in the 1956 elections it might be made clear that only those who were actively against the Mau Mau movement would be allowed to vote. If some definite proposals about the elections of African representatives for the next Council in 1956 were made *now*, it would, I think, have a very good effect indeed.

In the first place, it would show those tribes which have not actively participated in Mau Mau that Government is genuinely anxious that they should express their views in the Legislature through representatives chosen by themselves and in whom they have confidence. Secondly, the fact that the Kikuyu were only to have a limited vote, because of Mau Mau terrorism, would do a lot to prevent other tribes from ruining their chance of choosing their own representatives, by giving Mau Mau any support. Thirdly, if some definite statement of plans were to be issued fairly soon and well before 1956, it would give the tribes plenty of time to think about whom they wished to choose as their representatives, and even possibly to send likely candidates, who had an insufficient knowledge of English, overseas, so as to qualify them for candidature and possible election.

When Kikuyu and other Africans come to England, whether as students or on brief visits of a month or two, to improve their knowledge of the English language and to gain a wider background, much more could be done by people living in Great Britain to help them.

All too often they are left alone or even openly shunned by the decent, ordinary men and women in this country, so that they fall all the more easily to the blandishments of members of the communist party, who are all too keen to offer friendship and hospitality and win them over to their way of life.

If readers of this book seriously want to help in this way—and there is a very great deal they can do—I am sure that if they contacted the British Council and the Colonial Office organisations that deal with African students they would find their offers of help warmly welcomed. Moreover, they would be very amply rewarded by the new interests that such contacts would create.

The Kikuyu and other African peoples of Kenya are standing at the cross-roads. If we help them right now they will take a road of inter-social co-operation, if we fail them (or if we ourselves take the wrong turning now), then not only the future of Kenya, but the future of all Africa may be disastrous.

Personally, I have faith, complete faith, that wisdom and common sense will prevail and that the peoples of Kenya, black, white, and brown, will jointly show that it is possible to work together in harmony for the common good and progress of all.